NINE SWEET FRUITS

Nine sweet fruits

A life-study on the fruits of the Spirit

MARY LEE EHRLICH

Tyndale House
Publishers, Inc.
Wheaton, Illinois

LIBRARY OF CONGRESS
CATALOG CARD NUMBER 80-54494
ISBN 0-8423-4702-X, PAPER

FIRST PRINTING, APRIL 1981
PRINTED IN THE
UNITED STATES OF AMERICA.

I dedicate this book
to my Lord and Savior
who invited me
to join his family
and
walk with him
forever and ever!
Hallelujah!

CONTENTS

But when the Holy Spirit controls our lives
he will produce this kind of fruit in us:
love, joy, peace, patience, kindness, goodness, faithfulness,
gentleness and self-control
(Galatians 5:22).

FOREWORD

We first met Mary Lee and her family when they joined our congregation in 1963. They were new to California, having just moved here from Wisconsin where they had lived since their marriage in 1950. We did not know Mary Lee in the early years of her illness, but she was still very shy and insecure when we first met her at our church. She once said that she'd "never be able to get up in front of people to speak"—but we encouraged her to share what God had done in her life. Step by step we watched her grow in confidence as she hesitantly stepped out in faith—leaning on the inner power of our Lord. The more she experienced the positiveness of Christ in her own life, the more she was able to relate these truths to the women in our church. The deeper she searched God's Word for answers, the more spiritual insights she discovered.

Although she had a degree in education from the University of Wisconsin, Mary Lee continued to expand her religious education through our Lay Minister's Training Center. By 1973 she felt ready to offer her services as a Bible teacher in our Women's Department. We encouraged Mary Lee to come forward with a special Bible study centered on all the positiveness of Jesus Christ our Lord, for we had seen Mary Lee come from the depths of despair to an especially close walk with her Lord. Through searching the Scriptures and the commentaries of countless Bible scholars, she has compiled several inspiring and uplifting Bible studies. Hundreds of women have flocked to Mary Lee's classes and have found the positive answers to everyday living through her teaching.

Mary Lee continued her teaching ministry in our church for several years, writing her own creative Bible studies as she went along. She did a topical study entitled the "A.B.C.'s of Abundant Christian Living" that taught our women how to exchange their negative emotions for positive emotions by using Christ's cure in the Scriptures. She spent three years taking our women on a "Journey Through the Scriptures" (all sixty-six books in the Bible). As the women grew to love and cherish their Bibles, they wanted more, so Mary Lee wrote "God's Very Inspirational Persons," "Walking and Talking with Jesus," and "Walking in the Spirit." This last course of study was based on the Fruit of the Spirit. Because it was so effective in changing lives and deepening commitment, Mary Lee felt led to take a "spiritual sabbatical" for the purpose of putting these principles into book form.

Nine Sweet Fruits is the result. Readers will meet the living Christ in the pages of this book. They will have an opportunity to experience a "character transplant" as the Lord himself fills them with his personality traits of love, joy, peace, patience, kindness, goodness, faithfulness, gentleness, and self-control. Mary Lee's honest sharing of her own spiritual struggles and delightful discoveries will encourage the reader to lay claim to his or her divine inheritance as a child of God. Don't expect to be the same after reading this book. Through the many Scripture quotes that Mary Lee weaves throughout her book, you will meet Jesus face to face. Be sure to use the "Readers' Pages" at the back of the book to stimulate personal introspection and growth—or use them as a study guide for small groups in your family, church, or neighborhood.

We are grateful that, in the providence of time, God caused our paths to cross. Mary Lee is a yielded instrument in the Master's hands—so we have no doubt that he will use this book to spread his "Good News."

Bob and Arvella Schuller
Crystal Cathedral
Garden Grove, California

PREFACE

Nine Sweet Fruits is the outgrowth of a half century of *growing up* in the Lord. As a toddler I sang about him in Sunday school; as a teenager I heard about him at church camps and conferences; as a twenty-six-year-old I met him face to face through his "angels unaware"—family, friends, doctors, nurses, and therapists. They taught me about God's grace—God's love in action for people like me who felt terribly unworthy and totally hopeless.

For twenty-five years I had searched in vain to "find God." I had prayed in my upstairs closet, read my Bible, and tried to keep the Ten Commandments. I attended church twice on Sunday and once in the middle of the week, said all the "right words," but I never met Jesus along the way. I met other people who seemed to know him. I even asked them, "How?" One conference leader told me to "give myself to God" . . . so at age thirteen I found a private grassy slope under a big tree and I "gave God my mind, my eyes, my ears, my mouth, my hands, and my feet." I wrote down all my known sins on a piece of paper and threw it into the evening fire, as a symbol of turning my back on the "old me." I truly wanted to be a new person.

I had accepted the Lord that night, but what I did not know was that he had *also* accepted me. Thirty-seven years later, I now know that this "teenage transaction" was signed, sealed, and recorded in heaven. God knew the intentions of my heart even then, but I did not have any idea of my rich inheritance as a new member of God's family. I did not know that the Lord Jesus wanted to live his life through me. I did not know that he had sent his Holy Spirit to empower me with the delicious fruit of his Spirit—love, joy, peace, patience, kindness, goodness, faithfulness, gentleness, and self-control. I did not know that the Father loved me just as I was and had a special plan for my life—and a willingness to anoint me with unique gifts of the Spirit so I could carry out his plan.

And so for a long time I walked through this life not knowing he was right there beside me all the while. How often he must have whispered into my ear.:

"Mary Lee, let me love you so you can love yourself."

"Mary Lee, leave your mistakes with me so you can feel clean and forgiven."

"Mary Lee, lean on me so you can feel strong and confident."

"Mary Lee, learn about me. My Love Letter was written for you."

"Mary Lee, listen to me. I guide you when we converse with each other."

"Mary Lee, love my children (unconditionally—as I love you)."

"Mary Lee, lead your friends and loved ones to me. Put their hands in mine."

But I didn't hear God talking to me then. During those days of my life I was filled with sorrow, surrounded by guilt, caught in fear, confused about what to do, and swallowed up in inferiority. I kept sinking deeper and deeper into an emotional, mental, and physical state of exhaustion and failure. When I hit bottom, God's arms caught me and he carried me until I could walk on my own two feet again. But this time God and I would walk hand in hand forever.

The discoveries and insights I have made in this walk with my Lord are all recorded in this book with the prayer that many of God's children will find a shortcut to living life as it was meant to be. Ask the Lord to walk with you *today*. Don't wait another minute. Reach out and take his hand. He's been waiting for you a long, long time.

Yours and his,

Mary Lee

I thank . . .

My family
who accept and love me
"just as I am"—
surrounding me with their prayers.

My small group
of Christian brothers and sisters
who encourage me to respond
to God's plan for my life.

My Bible study ladies
who challenge me
to be an instrument
in the hands of the Lord.

My pastors, teachers, and doctors
who have inspired me
with their wisdom and insights

My girlfriend, Carol Bledsoe,
who graciously types all my lessons,
transcripts, and manuscripts.

"*To God be the Glory*!"

ONE
Taste the Fruit of LOVE

One night I had a dream—
I dreamed I was walking along the beach with the Lord and
Across the sky flashed scenes from my life.
For each scene I noticed two sets of footprints in the sand.
One belonged to me and the other to the Lord.
When the last scene of my life flashed before us,
I looked back at the footprints in the sand.
I noticed, that many times along the path of my life,
There was only one set of footprints,
I also noticed that it happened at the very lowest and saddest times in my life.
This really bothered me and I questioned the Lord about it.
"Lord, you said that once I decided to follow you,
You would walk with me all the way,
But I have noticed that during the most troublesome times in my life
There is only one set of footprints.
I don't understand why in times when I needed you most, you should leave me."
The Lord replied, "My precious, precious child. I love you and would never, never leave you during your times of trial and suffering.
When you saw only one set of footprints,
It was then that I carried you."[1]

"Footprints in the Sand," Author Unknown

Can you identify with this scene? Have you ever felt you were walking through life all alone, or have you always known that Jesus was walking with you? I must admit that I did not know this for over a quarter of a century.

My moment of crisis came at age twenty-six. I had been married five years, we had two sons, ages three and four, and I was falling apart at the seams.

I had dreamed of having a "storybook marriage." I had met my "Prince Charming" seven years before at the university, and after a two-year courtship, we had a big wedding in my hometown. We honeymooned in our nation's capital and settled down in our first apartment on the East Coast. But we didn't live happily ever after as I thought we would. Even on my wedding night I was scared to death of the total commitment that's involved in marriage. Then there were budgets and bills and babies and bottles and we had our share of arguments over these. And so I chalked it all up as a failure.

I had dreamed of being the "ideal mother" all my life. Nine months after our wedding I presented my husband with our first baby boy. Fifteen months later I presented him with our second baby boy. I read every book that was printed in those days and did everything they told me to do. I took the children for a daily walk in the park (even in our cold winters). I fed them three healthy meals a day, played with them, bathed them each night, read them a bedtime story, and tucked them in with prayers. And yet for some strange reason, they still argued with each other, bickered with each other, and talked back to me. What was I doing wrong? . . . another failure!

I had intended to become a "creative homemaker." I bought cookbooks and magazines filled with all those beautiful pictures. I'd follow the recipes step by step, but they never turned out like the pictures and I never got requests for a repeat performance. I tried my hand at sewing, but we ended up hiding the curtains on the back porch. Couldn't I do anything well? . . . another failure!

I decided to try to be the "perfect hostess." Early in the morning before a party I'd begin by cleaning out the refrigerator, scouring the stove, scrubbing floors, polishing furniture, preparing refreshments and games. But by the time the company arrived, I was ready to fall in a heap at their feet. I couldn't even enjoy them . . . another failure!

I had wanted God to be proud of me. And here I was crying over all my frustrations and failures, screaming at our children, arguing with my husband, and totally unable to live up to my dreams and desires. Even God must be ashamed of me! . . . another failure!

One summer night I decided to go to the movies by myself. *A Man Called Peter* was playing in our local theater. I had read the book and I was anxious to see it dramatized on the big screen. Little did I realize that what I was about to see would be the catalyst to open up a floodgate of hidden emotions. There before my very eyes, I saw everything I had ever dreamed about in a happy, Christ-centered marriage and family—filled with the visible fruit of the Spirit. A deep ache in my heart welled up. I began to sob and could not stop. A lifetime of idealistic dreams had been shattered and I saw no way out. Peter and Catherine Marshall had what I wanted, but I didn't know how to find it. My emotional turmoil and inner misery were more than I could stand.

It was at this point I began to suffer physical symptoms that sent me to our family physician. After a thorough exam he asked the penetrating question, "Are you happy, Mary Lee?" I hedged and told him, "Of course I am." But I went back home knowing something was miserably wrong. My physical symptoms continued, now compounded by emotional problems until I was no longer able to eat, sleep, or function as a wife and mother. Day after day my husband would come home from work to care for our little boys and take me to the doctor. The doctor tried to help with medication, the minister tried to help with counseling, and finally a psychiatrist tried to help with psychotherapy, but eventually hospitalization in a private sanitarium was recommended. One psychiatrist shook his head and said to my husband, "You might as well just put her in a sanitarium and start a new life for yourself, because I don't think she'll ever get well."

And so on a cold, snowy day we walked around and around our block trying to make a decision. Nothing else had worked, so what was left? We came home and packed my suitcase, left our two little boys with friends, and began the several hour drive to the private sanitarium. When we got there it was late at night and there was a psychiatrist waiting to talk to us. After he signed me in, he said to my husband and mother, "Say goodbye and the nurse will see Mary Lee to her room." I followed her up a flight of stairs and through several locked doors before walking down a long hall to my "new room." When I looked inside I found a room not much larger than our bathroom at home. I saw a metal bed, a metal chair, and a metal dresser. Across the windows were bars. I thought, "Oh, my goodness, I've landed in some kind of hell for the living dead!"

The nurse asked me to open my suitcase and check in all my clothes. One by one I handed them to her. When she saw my picture of our two little sons, she asked me to give it to her. I answered, "No, I want to put that on my dresser so I can remember what they look like." She replied, "Sorry, hospital rules!" Before she left, she took my left hand and asked me to give her my wedding ring. I pulled back and begged, "Oh, no, that's from my husband. You can't have that!" But once again she repeated those familiar words, "Sorry, hospital rules." By now I felt stripped naked. I really *was* a complete failure. Nobody trusted me anymore.

Before she turned to leave, she suggested I might want to stroll down the hall to the patient's lounge before going to sleep for the night. When I learned that the girl across the hall was living in a "world of fantasy" and when I saw some of the other patients standing alone in a corner talking to themselves, I became petrified. Was it just a matter of time until I became like one of them? All night long I tossed and turned to the cries of other patients calling for help.

I crawled out of bed on that cold, concrete floor. On my knees, I called out to God, "Help! I give up! Make me well!" I no longer felt worthy to even ask but it was at this moment, I am convinced, that I fell into his arms. My miracle of healing had begun and God was going to use his "angels unaware" to make me well.

Now, how did I come to this crisis point in my life? What had I done wrong? All my life I had been searching for God. I had read my Bible. I had prayed. I had gone to church and conferences. I said all the right words. I tried so hard to be good. Where was God? Didn't he hear me? I had accepted him when I was thirteen. Hadn't he accepted me? I tried to talk to him. Why didn't he talk to me? "Oh, my God," I thought. "Will I ever find you?"

Does this sound a little like Brother Paul when he said:

> I don't understand myself at all, for I really want to do what is right, but I can't. I do what I don't want to do—what I hate. I know perfectly well that what I am doing is wrong, and my bad conscience proves that I agree with these laws I am breaking. But I can't help myself, because I'm no longer doing it. It is sin inside me that is stronger than I am that makes me do these evil things. I know I am rotten through and through so far as my old sinful nature is concerned. No matter which way I turn I can't make myself do right. I want to but I can't. . . . I love to do God's will as far as my new nature is concerned, but there is something else deep within me, in my lower nature, that is at war with my mind and wins the fight and makes me a slave to the sin that is still within me. . . . Oh what a terrible predicament I'm in! Who will free me from my slavery to this deadly lower nature? [Portions of Romans 7].

And then Paul answers his own question, "Thank God! It has been done by Jesus Christ our Lord. He has set me free. So there is no condemnation awaiting those who belong to Christ Jesus. . . . He has freed me from the vicious circle of sin and death" (Rom. 7:25; 8:1, 2).

Ah . . . this is what I was about to learn in the weeks and months ahead. Even though I had considered myself a failure as a wife, mother, and child of God, God still loved me very much. And even though I made mistakes and did not always live up to my best intentions, he saw me as a forgiven sinner because of what Jesus Christ had done for me on the cross.

What I did not understand as a little girl and young woman growing up was that God's love is unconditional. He accepts us just where we are and then (with our cooperation) turns us into the kind of a person he wants us to be.

So all the time I was growing up, searching, and trying to "find God," he was right there all the time . . . only I didn't know it. He wanted to love me, but I didn't know how to let him love me.

When I lost my baby brother, he wanted to comfort me!

When I broke my desk and tried to hide it, he wanted to forgive me!

When I was frightened in an electric storm, he wanted to reassure me!

When I didn't know how to act on a date, he wanted to show me!

When I failed as a wife and mother, he wanted to teach me!

When I was ashamed of myself, he wanted to give me a new image!

So this is where we all must begin . . . with the love and mercy of God. "God's riches at Christ's expense" spells G-R-A-C-E, and that's what I had to learn about. I knew about Eros-love (sexual love) and I knew about Phileo-love (brotherly love), but I did not know about Agape-love and Hesid-love (love that never gives up) . . . love that was willing to go to the cross for me and never give up on me. Where do you meet this kind of love? Can you see it, feel it, experience it, touch it? Can you run into its arms? Two thousand years ago you could, for Jesus came to earth to show us that God is love. In those days people could actually come up to the Lord and he would physically put his arm around them and bless them. He would lay his hands upon their heads and take little children upon his lap. But today, Jesus is living in heaven, so how can we run into his arms of love? Very simply! Fifty days after his resurrection and ascension into heaven, his Holy Spirit was released into this world to live inside all believers. This event was called Pentecost and we are still living in the age of spirit-filled believers. These are the people who yield their bodies to the Holy Spirit.

. . . Jesus smiles through their eyes.

. . . Jesus listens through their ears.

. . . Jesus speaks through their lips.

. . . Jesus touches through their hands.

. . . Jesus loves through their hearts.

THE FRUIT OF LOVE

Love is the foundation stone of everything. The Scriptures say that love is eternal. It's going to last forever. When we die and go to live with the Lord, we're going to actually sit at the feet of Love. We're going to be able to see Love with our eyes, hear Love with our ears, and touch Love with our hands, because we will be in heaven with Jesus. But in the meantime, down here on Planet Earth, we can experience God's love in action through human beings who give unselfishly of themselves to others. This is what began to happen to me in the sanitarium when I was twenty-six years old.

God sent a doctor the morning after I was admitted to the sanitarium who said, "I know you don't believe you'll get well, but I do; so believe me." And with that he gave me back my little boy's picture and my wedding ring.

God sent me to a different wing in the hospital where I was less afraid and he provided nurses who encouraged and challenged me to get out of bed, comb my hair, join an exercise class, make craft projects for my family, participate in a puppet show, play the piano, and serve trays to patients who were too sick to care. They gave me unconditional love and taught me how to give it back to others.

God sent occupational and physical therapists into my life who would not give up on me when I said, "No, I can't do it!" They said, "Sure you can," and showed me how.

God sent my husband to visit every weekend and the doctor gave us "weekend passes" to rediscover and court each other. We were learning to laugh again and it was not until it was time for him to leave that I would cry and beg him, "Take me home with you!" But because of his love he would say, "No, not yet, honey."

God sent my mother and my husband's mother to take turns caring for our two little boys. They provided the stability our sons had not known for a long time and in the process they grew more secure and less upset.

God encouraged our boys to draw pictures and print little notes with the help of their daddy and grandmas and these became my "dessert" every day if I would agree to eat all the food on my tray.

So what is this kind of love? When the Scriptures say, "Love each other just as much as I love you," what is in-

volved? Let's look at some attributes of love:
...Love is positive!
...Love builds people up!
...Love is unconditional!
...Love compliments!
...Love forgives!
...Love heals!
...Love is patient!
...Love asks the right questions!
...Love is profoundly simple!
...Love never gives up!

There are many, many more attributes. Reread 1 Corinthians 13:4-7 several times a day until Paul's words about "agape love" sink deep into your subconscious.

> Love is very patient and kind, never jealous or envious, never boastful or proud, never haughty or selfish or rude. Love does not demand its own way. It is not irritable or touchy. It does not hold grudges and will hardly even notice when others do it wrong. It is never glad about injustice, but rejoices whenever truth wins out. If you love someone you will be loyal to him no matter what the cost. You will always believe in him, always expect the best of him, and always stand your ground in defending him.

And then reread what Paul says in Ephesians 3:17-19 about being filled up with the love of God:

> I pray that Christ will be more and more at home in your hearts, living within you as you trust in him. May your roots go down deep into the soil of God's marvelous love, and may you be able to feel and understand, as all God's children should, how long, how wide, how deep, and how high his love really is; and to experience this love for yourselves, though it is so great that you will never see the end of it or fully know or understand it. And so at least you will be filled up with God himself.

And if you doubt that God could possible love you, reread Paul's words in Romans 8:38, 39:

> I am convinced that nothing can ever separate us from his [God's] love. Death can't, and life can't. The angels won't, and all the powers of hell itself cannot keep

> God's love away. Our fears for today, our worries about tomorrow, or where we are—high above the sky, or in the deepest ocean—nothing will ever be able to separate us from the love of God demonstrated by our Lord Jesus Christ when he died for us.

This is the kind of love I was beginning to experience in my hospital room and this is the kind of love that was going to follow me home and back into our church and neighborhood. Let me share a few illustrations.

LOVE IS POSITIVE

After three months in the hospital, my doctors agreed to let me try it at home on my own with weekly outpatient therapy. Our attitude was positive. "With God's help, we can do it."

We set some definite goals as a family. We would play together more and enjoy each other. After being apart for so long this was not difficult to do. We went on weekend fishing trips at a nearby lake, we had backyard picnics and waded in our little plastic pool. We bought a used upright player piano and sang songs and played musical games after dinner. We tucked the boys in bed with "conversational prayers," speaking to God as we would speak to a friend right there in the room with us. God began to answer our simple, specific prayers and in the process he became more and more real to all of us.

LOVE BUILDS PEOPLE UP

One day I felt myself slipping back into depression. Would I have to go back to the sanitarium? I was watching my little boy build a block tower, when he noticed me sitting over in the corner. He came over to me and started tugging at my hand, "Come on, Mommy, help me build." And so I moved over next to him. He turned to me and smiled, saying, "I don't mean just watch me build, I mean *help* me build." And with these words he took my hand, placed it on a block and lifted the block to the top of his tower. And my heart wept inside at the compassion of such a tiny little boy. Already he knew how "to build people up." To this day he is still the compassionate soul he was at three.

LOVE IS UNCONDITIONAL

"For better or for worse. . . . in sickness or in health. . . ." the wedding vows had said. My husband was certainly living up to those words. Some days I was better, other days I seemed worse. Some days I was healthy, other days I was physically or emotionally sick. But it didn't seem to matter. On those days when he reminded me of our goal to play more with the children, I would sometimes say, "Oh, not today, I have things to do in the house." But he wouldn't take no for an answer. More than once he put on my jacket, pulled on my boots, and gently dragged me out in the snow to build a snowman, go tobogganing, or have a snowball fight. When I didn't want to live again, he *made* me live again. That's unconditional love!

LOVE COMPLIMENTS

How can you say anything nice about a person who can't cook or sew or do anything very well? God had a solution. He used two different neighbors who loved to cook and sew to teach me how. Now it wasn't easy, because I used to hide behind my curtains and just peek out at my neighbors, wishing I could be more like them. But they did not let me stay behind my curtains. They found all kinds of interesting "excuses" to ring my doorbell. Eventually I felt comfortable with them and before I knew what was happening, there I was in their kitchen and living room making bread and knitting a baby sweater. They told me what a "good job" I was doing and I began to believe them and try out my new "experiments" at home. More compliments came, and my self-confidence began to grow.

LOVE FORGIVES

I hated myself for getting sick and causing my family so much heartache. Sometimes I wanted to run away and give them peace and freedom to make a new life for themselves. I never considered suicide because I was already living in a mental hell on earth and I feared if I took my own life there might be an eternity of this kind of existence. I did consider finding a job in some Salvation Army house in the slums and working myself to death so I could die legitimately, but I never seemed to have the physical energy to leave. Time after time I would apologize for my slow recovery, but always I was assured they were "so happy to have me home." My family seemed to forgive my weaknesses and encourage my accomplishments. When I told my doctor how much more I used to be able to do when I was well, he insisted I was to congratulate myself on each job I completed, no matter how small it was. I was not supposed to "put myself down" anymore. I was to forgive myself and accept myself—the same way God did.

LOVE HEALS

After many months of doing things alone as a family, my doctor said I was ready to try going out with my husband to office functions. I was scared to death it wouldn't work, but I still had a lot to learn about the healing side of love. One night we were at a house party. Everybody was having a good time laughing and talking. They treated me like "one of them," not like some lady who just got out of the hospital. When it came time for dessert and coffee, I wondered what I would do because I was unable to tolerate caffeine. I was still too embarrassed to share the truth. But somehow our hostess knew, for when she handed me my cup I noticed it was filled with warm milk (like I was used to drinking at bedtime). Nobody else even noticed and I smiled a warm "thank you" to my understanding friend.... Another friend insisted I join her once a week for a "Girl's Night Out at the Y." Exercise is an excellent "healing source" for people who suffer from depression. She knew this and her willingness to go with me every week amazed me. I was also learning how to talk "girl talk," something I had been too shy to try before. God was at work healing my tense body and tight emotions.

LOVE IS PATIENT

Our friends at church did not pressure me back into "church work." They knew I was embarrassed about what had happened to me and they wanted to make it as easy as possible for me to return. The first job I volunteered for was playing the piano for the preschoolers. I turned and faced the piano and the tunes were simple enough. One day I got up enough nerve to turn around and teach them a finger-play. They liked it and that added another ounce of self-confidence. From this point on they let me experiment with other jobs whenever I felt ready. Step by step God was "growing me" into an instrument of his grace.

LOVE ASKS THE RIGHT QUESTIONS

When I played the piano for the children, they responded enthusiastically, so obviously I found a niche where God could use me. When I scraped plates in the kitchen and served at the tables, I felt comfortable because I didn't have to face a lot of people. But when I baked a pie or cake for the bake sale, it was usually left over for my husband to buy. Obviously this was not one of my strong points.

When I took a job as treasurer, I had trouble with my arithmetic and stammered when I tried to read my report aloud. Obviously this was not my special "gift" either. When I took over the ordering and purchasing for Sunday school supplies, my poor husband ended up having to keep the books, so obviously this still wasn't the right spot for me.

And then one day some couples helped me discover a gift I wasn't aware I had. Maybe I couldn't cook up a storm or make pretty curtains or keep good books; but wow, was it *fun* to study God's Word and turn it into a creative Bible study for others. Soon I was writing little plays, putting together devotionals, and leading a women's study group. The more I explored God's Love Letter, the more questions I got answered. God was teaching me so I could someday teach others.

LOVE IS PROFOUNDLY SIMPLE

This was one of the most exciting insights of all. Love was not complicated. The door latch into the Kingdom of God was low enough for even me to reach.

I had felt weak and useless, but the Lord said to me, "My power shows up best in weak people" (2 Cor. 12:9). Then I would know beyond a shadow of a doubt that I was leaning on God and not on my own resources. I really could "do all things through him who strengthened me" (Phil. 4:13). (How simple . . . just let Christ live his life through me!)

I had felt guilty and unworthy, but the Lord said to me, "I accept and acquit you. I declare you 'not guilty' if you trust Jesus Christ to take away your sins. All can be saved in this same way no matter who they are or what they have been like" (Rom. 3:22). (How simple . . . just trust and he forgives my sins!)

I had felt like such a failure, but the Lord said to me, "Because of your faith, God has brought you into this place of highest privilege where you now stand. You can confidently and joyfully look forward to actually becoming all that God has had in mind for you to be" (Rom. 5:2). (How simple . . . just let him do it for me!)

God was going to take over the reins of my life. I could stop struggling and fighting. I could relax and make myself available for him to use any way he wanted. Living the Christian life meant there was supernatural power available to me. I didn't have to run life under my own steam anymore. What a relief! Life was not as complicated as I had thought it to be.

LOVE NEVER GIVES UP

Does this mean our problems are over? Does this mean we'll never slip again? Of course not. People still get sick and die. People get hurt and suffer pain. Husbands still walk out on wives and wives walk out on husbands. Children still run away from home and rebel against their parent's teachings. Catastrophes still occur. But something *new* has been added when we "walk with Jesus." Then we can throw our shoulders back and hold our heads up high and say with Brother Paul:

> We are pressed on every side by troubles, *but* not crushed and broken. We are perplexed because we don't know why things happen as they do, *but* we don't give up and quit. We are hunted down, *but* God never abandons us. We get knocked down, *but* we get up again and keep going [2 Cor. 4:8, 9].

How do we get this kind of love inside us? Where do we find it? I had tried to "make" it happen by sheer willpower. I lived by the "bootstrap theory" until I wore myself out. It wasn't until I fell into the arms of Love that I discovered there was another way—a much easier way. God's way.

Not everyone has to learn this lesson the hard way like I did, but on the other hand, some never learn there *is* such a gift as "divine love." They've never heard about it or they've never seen it demonstrated. Still others are *afraid* to let God love them. They draw back because they do not understand God's grace. Brother John knew this when he wrote:

> We need have no fear of someone who loves us perfectly; his perfect love for us eliminates all dread of what he might do to us. If we are afraid, it is for fear of what he might do to us, and shows that we are not fully convinced that he really loves us. So you see, our love for him comes as a result of his loving us first [1 John 4:18, 19].

I understand this very well, for we adopted a little girl from Korea when she was only three years old. She had lived with her mother for two and one-half years and in the orphanage for six months. So we were her third home in three years. We looked different, spoke a different language, ate different, and slept different. We were strangers to her, so she put up a protective shield. She would not let us love her or cuddle her or comfort her. We had to win her love day by day, hour by hour. She finally decided to love us because we first loved her. She learned she could trust us with her life. That's the same as it is with us and God. When we finally decide to respond to his love and open our hearts to his Holy Spirit, he moves deeply within our very soul. Then we can begin to walk with him in love.

Ask Jesus to fill you with the fruit of his Holy Spirit so you can understand *his love* and let it overflow to others.

TWO
Taste the Fruit of JOY

Do you walk with Jesus or are you missing the *joy* of your salvation? Do you walk through life with a bounce in your step and a sparkle in your eye, or do you plug along day in and day out? Do your moods shift from high to low? Is there another fruit of the Spirit available to God's children? If God's love can convince us we're very special to him, what can God's joy do for us? How do we get it and what is it like?

Jesus suggests in his Word that joy awaits us when we talk with him. But we never seem to have the time. We're always running here and there. And yet he waits—morning, noon, and night—hoping we will notice him and stop to visit.

Why do we rush about like we do? Why are our calendars so crowded with "things to do"? Why don't we take time to sit down and be quiet? What keeps us from visiting with Jesus on a daily basis? How is it with our earthly friends?

...Do you enjoy a surprise phone call from a friend?

...Do you enjoy a letter from a loved one?

...Do you enjoy a neighborhood or office "coffee break"?

...Do you enjoy it when your children sit still long enough to talk with you?

Well, it's no different with the Lord! He, too, enjoys it when we stop everything and give him our undivided attention. Oh sure, we can shoot up prayers while we move about our daily tasks, but the best times are when we get comfortable, sit down, and say, "Let's talk, Lord." Listen to what Jesus says about these conversations. "Ask, using my name, and you will receive, and your cup of *joy* will overflow" (John 16:24).

Would you like your "cup of joy" to overflow? Then do what he says, talk with the Father using Jesus' name. But what does that mean?

...It means that you can *know* God personally when you pray in his Son's name.

...It means that your prayer requests will be *in line* with the Father's will when you pray in Jesus' name.

...It means that the Holy Spirit will pray *for you* when you pray in Jesus' name.

For you see, "name" refers to the total character of God. When we look at Jesus we know what the Father is like. When we pray in Jesus' name, the Holy Spirit unites our spirit with the Father and we experience unspeakable joy.

But only God's children can pray in Jesus' name and really mean it, for as the Scriptures say, "No one can say, 'Jesus is Lord' and really mean it, unless the Holy Spirit is helping him" (1 Cor. 12:3). And no one can have the Holy Spirit's help in praying until they first accept Christ, but, "Anyone who calls upon the name of the Lord will be saved" (Rom. 10:13). So it's really very simple. *Call* on his name, and then *pray* in his name.

Praying in Jesus' name makes it possible for you to walk with the Lord in joy. Do you believe this? Is this really true? Does it always work? You say:

"Yes, when life is running smoothly.
Yes, when relationships are peaceful.
Yes, when everybody is healthy and happy."

But, how about those time of stress and strain?

...those times of sorrow?

...those times of guilt and disappointment?

...those times of disobedience?

...those times of confusion and frustration?

Does it work then? Can a Christian's "cup of joy" overflow in times like these? Let's look at a few illustrations.

JOY IN THE MIDST OF SORROW

What happens when we lose a loved one—the phone rings, a telegram comes, or someone knocks on the door to deliver the news? What goes on inside of us?

First, we are in a state of shock—our insides scream out, "No, no, no."

Second, we are in a state of disbelief—"This isn't for real, it's just a bad dream."

Third, we are in a state of rebellion—"Why, Lord? Why did this happen to me?"

Fourth, we are in a state of confusion, as we alternate between depression and anxiety—"How can I go on living? How can I face tomorrow?"

My first experience with sorrow came when I was only five years of age. I had been praying for a baby brother and God answered. He sent our family a darling baby boy, but eight weeks later he took him back home to heaven. This was very difficult for me to understand. When my baby brother first got sick with spinal meningitis, I bargained with God in prayer, "Make him well and I promise to never forget my bedtime prayers again."

When he was not healed, I got mad at God and felt "guilty" for having such "bad thoughts." There was *no more joy* in my heart. I continued to cry on the inside long after I stopped crying on the outside.

In the years that followed, I lost my favorite uncle, followed by my grandparents, and other relatives and friends. If I had only understood and believed that, "Anyone who believes in me, even though he dies like anyone else, shall live again" (John 11:26). If I had only had the assurance that I would see my loved ones in a very real place called heaven, then I could have experienced a "future joy" in the midst of my sorrow. This was the kind of "joy" Jesus was talking about to his disciples just before his crucifixion when he said:

> Your weeping shall suddenly be turned to wonderful *joy* [when you see me again]. It will be the same *joy* as that of a woman in labor when her child is born—her anguish gives place to rapturous *joy* and the pain is

> forgotten. You have sorrow now, but I will see you again and then you will *rejoice; and no one can rob you of that joy* [John 16:20-22].

By the time my daddy fell asleep on earth and woke up in heaven, I was thirty-three years of age and for seven years Jesus had been whispering into my ear from out of the pages of his Word. I still went through stage one (shock) and stage two (disbelief) but his Holy Spirit short-circuited stages three (rebellion) and four (confusion) so that they were not nearly as intense. Oh, I still cried out, "Why, God, when we were just getting ready to move to California together?" And I wondered how life could ever be the same without Daddy, but very quickly the heavenly Father began to comfort me with the assurance of Scripture . . . with the promise of seeing my daddy again. All of a sudden heaven became more real than it had ever been before. Daddy was free of pain and running all over God's green heaven. Now I could agree with Brother Paul when he said:

> Every moment we spend in these earthly bodies is time spent away from our eternal home in heaven with Jesus. . . . And we are not afraid, but are quite content to die, for then we will be at home with the Lord [2 Cor. 5:6-8].

Daddy was now "at home with the Lord." I could rejoice for him and look forward to our reunion. Yes, when we walk with the Lord, we can even experience "joy" in the midst of our sorrow. On the day of my father's "graduation service," we felt the tender loving touch of our heavenly Comforter. Jesus' promise in the Beatitudes was true. "Those who mourn are fortunate, for they shall be comforted" (Matt. 5:4).

JOY IN THE PRESENCE OF GUILT

Wait a minute, how could that be possible? I've never felt more miserable than when I was swallowed up in guilt. How about you? Would you agree? When you know you've done something wrong, it saps all the joy out of your life. Think back with me to those times in your life when you were flooded with guilt.

THE FRUIT OF JOY

When I was ten years old, I broke the pencil ledge on my school desk and tried to hide it for a whole year so it would not be discovered during desk check. I knew there was a fine for destroying school property so I lived in a state of guilt for a long, long time. I told no one and buried the secret deep within me. It took away all my joy in living. That broken desk loomed like a monster in the back of my mind and made it impossible for me to really laugh and have a good time with the other children.

Did you know that we were not meant to live with guilt? Nobody is! Little children and big adults need to confess their guilt and be forgiven before their "joy in living" can return. Brother David, in the Old Testament, knew this all too well when he committed the sins of adultery and murder. Listen to his words about confession and forgiveness:

> Oh, wash me and cleanse me from this guilt. . . . Wash me and I shall be whiter than snow. And after you have punished me, give me back my *joy* again. . . . Restore to me again the *joy* of your salvation and make me willing to obey you [Portion of Psalm 51].
>
> What happiness for those whose guilt has been forgiven! What *joys* when sins are covered over! What relief for those who have confessed their sins and God has cleared their record [Portion of Psalm 32].

But I did not understand about confession and forgiveness when I was a child of ten. And before I learned about confession and forgiveness, I was to encounter other situations and experiences that added to my "guilt complex."

. . . I played hooky from school and signed my mother's name to my excuse.

. . . I smoked a cigarette and a younger girl who saw me thought, "If she can, so can I." (I quit, she continued.)

. . . I forgot to latch the stair gate and my neighbor's little boy fell down.

. . . I failed to repair a torn bedspread hem and my mother caught her foot in it and fell and broke her shoulder.

These are just a few, I'm sure there are many more. Whether it's an intentional or an unintentional action that causes guilt to rise up in our spirit, we need to turn to God's grace for forgiveness and cleansing. Just as a fever tells us our body is sick and needs attention, so guilt tells us our spirit is sick and needs God's attention. Then the "joy of our salvation" can return. Brother John tells us:

> My little children, . . . if you sin, there is someone to plead for you before the Father. His name is Jesus Christ, the one who is all that is good and who pleases God completely. He is the one who took God's wrath against our sins upon himself, and brought us into fellowship with God; and he is the forgiveness for our sins, and not only ours but all the world's [1 John 2:1, 2].

If we did not have the ability to feel guilt when we have sinned, then we would have no need to say, "I'm sorry." And without repentance there can be no forgiveness. A man or woman who has repeatedly rejected God and rationalized his sinful behavior, hardens his heart to the point of no longer recognizing the difference between good and evil. So keep the channels clear. Don't let guilt pile up. A simple and sincere "I'm sorry" from the heart is heard by God, and his Son wipes the slate clean. The "joy of our salvation" returns and we can smile again. So there we have it in a nutshell . . . guilt drives us to grace and grace restores our joy. Now we can stand before the Father in our clean, white robe of righteousness because of what Jesus did for us. Oh, what joy!

JOY IN THE MIDST OF OBEDIENCE

If sorrow and guilt can rob us of our joy, so can disobedience. Listen to what Jesus whispers into our ear from the pages of his Love Letter:

> When you obey me you are living in my love, just as I obey my Father and live in his love. I have told you this so that you will be filled with my *joy*. Yes, your cup of joy will overflow! [John 15:10, 11]

There it is again . . . our cup of joy will overflow! Does your cup of joy overflow? If not, is it possible that there might be something *you* have to do in order to "enjoy all that joy" that the Holy Spirit wants to pour into you? Well, the Scriptures call it "obedience." From the very beginning of time, the heavenly Father has been teaching us that his "laws of love" are fashioned for our own good. When we obey them, we discover built-in blessings, but when we disobey them, we discover built-in consequences. Do you find this true in your own life's experiences? I certainly do. Sometimes I wish we weren't such slow learners.

I know that if I begin my day with the Lord in Bible reading, prayer, and meditation, the day will go much better, but sometimes I forget and rush ahead with my agenda. My day doesn't run as smoothly and I know something is missing.

I know that if I eat healthy, nutritious foods I will feel better, but sometimes I munch on junk foods and pay the consequences of extra pounds or indigestion.

I know that I require sufficient rest and relaxation to function at my best, but sometimes I burn the candle at both ends and suffer the consequences of a headache or a cranky spirit.

I know that if I keep up with my household chores, I won't get behind or overloaded, but sometimes I let things pile up and I reap the bitter results.

I know that if I spend quality time with my husband and children, our relationships will grow richer, but sometimes I get busy doing my own thing and our communication suffers in the process.

I learned all these "lessons" in my late twenties when we nearly lost everything we held dear. But that doesn't mean I never slip back into some of my bad habit patterns. We all have to constantly check and recheck our priorities. So let's ask Jesus to help us do this. Let's invite him into our home and ask him to clean up every single room—from the attic to the basement. Take Jesus with you through every room of your house and dialogue with him. Listen carefully to his questions and responses and learn some valuable lessons from what he has to say. His words of wisdom are guaranteed to bring joy into every room of your home. If you listen and obey . . .

. . . Your kitchens will sparkle with laughter.

. . . Your living rooms will glow with love.

...Your family rooms will gleam with joy.
...Your bedrooms will become a sanctuary of peace.

As the Lord Jesus moves into the rooms of your home, let him also move into the rooms of your heart. Let him look deep, deep inside of you—way down into your subconscious memories. If there is any unpleasant thought, or resentment, or hurt, or grief, or guilt, let him have it. Let him fling it as far as the east is from the west. Let him bury it in the deepest ocean for, as the Scriptures promise, there is great joy when you walk and talk with the Lord each and every day.

Ask Jesus to fill you with the fruit of his Holy Spirit so you can experience *his joy* and let it overflow onto others.

THREE
Taste the Fruit of PEACE

I am leaving you with a gift—peace of mind and heart! And the peace I give isn't fragile like the peace the world gives. So don't be troubled or afraid [John 14:27].

THE WORLD'S PEACE

What does Jesus mean about "the world's peace" being fragile? Mr. Webster answers that for us in his dictionary when he says,

"Peace is freedom from war or civil strife. . . .
Peace is an agreement to end war. . . .
Peace is harmony—security—calm—quiet."

Pretty "fragile" wouldn't you agree? One look at the daily newspaper and evening TV tells us that:

. . . somewhere in the world people are fighting and killing one another;

. . . peace treaties are being broken;

. . . innocent people are being murdered on the streets;

. . . homes are being shattered with arguments, angry words, separation, and divorce.

Loud noises continually bombard our peace and quiet. Sonic booms shake our homes, motorcycles zoom down our streets, TVs blare, and electrical appliances whiz and whir around us.

GOD'S PEACE

So what kind of peace was Jesus talking about in John 14:27? What kind of "gift" does he want to give us? He says his gift of peace is twofold: It is peace of mind, (which is mental health) and it is peace of heart (which is emotional health).

Then he goes on to say, "Don't be troubled or afraid." Do you need this kind of peace? Do you want this kind of peace? I sure do!

Recently God has been teaching me how to receive and enjoy this gift of peace. First of all he introduced me to the beautiful Hebrew word for peace—"Shalom." Like the lovely Hawaiian word "Aloha," it has a multitude of meanings. Let's look at a few.

SHALOM MEANS TRANQUILITY (PERSONAL PEACE)

Back in the Old Testament days, the Lord gave Moses a beautiful blessing for the children of Israel:

> May the Lord bless and protect you; may the Lord's face radiate with joy because of you; may he be gracious to you, show you his favor, and give you his *peace* [Num. 6:25].

Today many Christian churches have adapted this Jewish blessing into their closing benediction. It states very clearly that God is the giver of peace. He is the one who will bless and protect us as we walk through this life. His is the only peace that will last forever! He backs it up with his divine mercy and justice. We need never be "troubled" or "afraid" again. The past, present, and future are in his capable hands.

SHALOM MEANS UNITY AMONG BELIEVERS (HORIZONTAL PEACE)

The Body of Christ is made up of men, women, and children who have invited the Lord into their lives. This Family of God is very special. Each person has a unique role to play. Together we are Christ's eyes, ears, lips, hands, and feet here on earth. It is very important that we support, uphold, and cooperate with one another if the Body of Christ is to function as a whole. Listen to Brother Paul's admonition to believers,

> Let the *peace* of heart which comes from Christ be always present in your hearts and lives—for this is your responsibility and privilege as members of his body [Col. 3:15].

There it is again . . . peace is a "gift" from Christ and God expects us to use it. Not only is it our responsibility, but it's also our privilege. If we keep peace in our hearts, we will experience a happy unity within the Body of Christ.

...We need to remember this when a brother or sister in the Lord "tries" our patience.

...We need to remember this when others in the church don't agree with our suggestions.

...We need to remember this when we don't feel appreciated.

...We need to remember this when the pastor or church leaders display their "feet of clay."

...We need to remember this when somebody gets more attention than we do.

...We need to remember this when a brother or sister in the Lord gets the job we wanted.

SHALOM MEANS RESTORED HARMONY (VERTICAL PEACE)

Not only does God's peace bring us personal tranquility and group unity, but it also restores harmony with the Father. No longer do we feel like drawing back in shame. We can face our Lord and walk with him hand in hand. Restored harmony brings peace with God—thanks to Jesus.

STUMBLING BLOCKS TO PEACE

Why would anyone ever refuse this gift? Why would we find it difficult to accept? What might be the stumbling blocks to receiving and enjoying God's gift of peace? If Jesus wants to give us sound mental and emotional health, why don't we

take it? Because we are too often filled with fear, guilt, and anger. These emotions clog up our channels and prevent us from receiving peace. So what do we do then? Do we just:
...ignore our feelings?
...tell them to go away?
...act like they don't exist?

No, we "talk them over" with the Lord and a brother or sister in the faith. We bring our feelings up to the surface and deal with them in broad daylight. It is true that "feelings are not facts" and "feelings are neither right nor wrong in themselves"; but, they *do exist* and they *must* be recognized and dealt with in a positive way. Let me share why.

DON'T HIDE YOUR FEELINGS

When I decided as a young child to "hide" my "bad" feelings and "pretend" like they didn't exist, I began a habit that robbed me of peace and tranquility. I buried my fear, guilt, and anger so deep that when it came forth in anxiety, depression, and disguised physical symptoms, I had no idea where it came from.

This is when we need to "talk it over" and "pray it through." Sometimes you and the Divine Physician can do it alone as you study the Word and explore two-way prayer together. Sometimes you can be helped to see yourself more clearly in group therapy. Other times you need the help of a "man of God"—a pastor, a counselor, a psychologist, or a psychiatrist. Together with the Holy Spirit's help you will discover insights that will make it possible for you to nip any future anger, fear, or guilt in the bud, before it has an opportunity to take root and entangle you in its grip.

NIP BITTERNESS IN THE BUD

There's a profound and penetrating verse found in Hebrews 12:15 that says:

> Look after each other so that not one of you will fail to find God's best blessings. Watch out that no *bitterness* takes root among you, for as it springs up it causes deep

trouble, hurting many in their spiritual lives.

This is 100 percent accurate! It has proven itself true in my life and I am sure it's been the same in your life. This Scripture tells us that:

1. When we are concerned about the *emotional needs* of others, we will *both* be blessed in the process.
2. When we deal positively with our own bitterness towards self (manifested as *guilt*) and towards others (manifested as *anger*), we prevent it from taking root and destroying us.
3. Unresolved emotions will not only cause *us* deep trouble, but they will hurt *others* as well.

So there we have it in Scripture. "No man is an island unto himself." We are all interrelated on this planet whether we like it or not. We do influence one another. Even though we may try and isolate ourselves from others, we can never totally separate ourselves from the positive and negative influences around us. Psychologists tell us that inside each one of us there are many voices and experiences that have shaped the way we act and react today. Many of our attitudes and habits were formed a long time ago and we often find ourselves reverting to these "old ways" of responding. For every "healthy pattern" we have learned and developed, we are richly blessed; but for every "unhealthy pattern" we have learned and developed, we are deeply miserable. The personal peace, horizontal peace, and vertical peace we talked about earlier are sadly missing when we react to life with unhealthy attitudes and reactions. But the encouraging promise is that *Christians can change* by yielding themselves to the Holy Spirit.

If we do not learn how to handle the traumatic experiences of life in a healthy, positive way, then those "terrible twins" of *anxiety* and *depression* will strike us. When that happens, our peace of mind and heart disappears and we feel as if we have landed in some kind of hell for the "living dead!"

I know because I've been there! Thank goodness it wasn't a one-way ticket! Mine was a "round-trip" to hell and back and I never want to go there again. There is no peace there!

LOVE, JOY, AND PEACE

In the chapter on love, I shared with you how God surrounded me with unconditional love during my healing process. He taught me how to love by putting me on the "receiving end" for awhile. Do you know someone who needs that kind of love? Maybe it's you. Let God love you! Let others love you.

In the chapter on joy, I shared with you how God taught me to "fill my cup with joy" even in the midst of sorrow (by letting him comfort and assure me); even in the midst of sin (by letting him cleanse and forgive me); and, especially in the midst of living (by choosing to obey his wise laws of love). Do you know anybody who needs to "fill his cup of joy?" Maybe it's you. Lift your cup now! In this chapter, I'd like to share with you how God is helping me appropriate his *gift of peace.*

PRESCRIPTION FOR PEACE

First of all, Jesus gave me a "Scripture prescription" to help break my unhealthy cycle of fear and anxiety.

> Don't worry about anything; instead pray about everything. Tell God your needs and don't forget to thank him for his answers. If you do this you will experience *God's peace* which is far more wonderful than the human mind can understand. His *peace* will keep your thoughts and your *hearts* quiet and at rest as you trust in Christ Jesus [Phil. 4:6, 7].

There it is again! Peace in our thoughts (mental health), and peace in our hearts (emotional health). Oh, how much he loves us and wants the best for us! But this Scripture also sets up some conditions on our part:

1. We need to stop worrying and start praying.
2. We need to thank God for his answers.
3. We need to trust Jesus to keep us quiet and at rest.

Can anybody do this by a sheer act of will? Maybe for a little while, but not forever. No, we need some *supernatural assistance* in order to live this way.

We must first belong to the Family of God, because God's supernatural gifts of love, joy, and peace come only through the Holy Spirit's presence in our lives. Until we realize this we will never be able to appropriate the fruit of the Spirit. So let's pause just a moment to look at Jesus' eight-point plan for salvation and sanctification.

We Need To:

1. Admit we don't have all the answers to life and ask for outside help. (*"Help me!"*)
2. Reject our old way of life and turn to God. (*"Forgive me!"*)
3. Invite Jesus into our hearts. (*"Take me!"*)
4. Hunger and thirst for spiritual growth. (*"Teach me!"*)
5. Ask Jesus for a "new spirit." (*"Fill me!"*)
6. Reflect Jesus in our words and actions. (*"Mold me!"*)
7. Take Christ's peace wherever we go. (*"Use me!"*)
8. Stand strong for Christ. (*"Empower me!"*)

(These steps into Christian maturity are based on Jesus' blessed Beatitudes from his Sermon on the Mount found in Matthew 5.)

For fifty years now he has been taking me through these eight steps. I have learned that *peace* comes near the end of the list after we've learned to surrender, confess, study the Word, pray, and yield ourselves as an instrument in God's hands. We must allow Christ's peace to sink deep down into our own hearts and minds before we can pass it on to others.

PRAY—THANK AND TRUST

This is where the "Scripture prescription" in Philippians 4:6, 7 comes in handy for God's children. I can't think of a more powerful prescription for producing peace.

Pray about everything.

Thank God for his answers.

Trust Jesus with our mental and emotional health.

The more we put Philippians 4:6, 7 into practice, the more it will become a permanent part of our personalities. Let's look at these insights one at a time and let me share with you what God has been teaching me.

PRAYING ABOUT EVERYTHING BRINGS PEACE

One of my greatest fears after losing my baby brother, uncle, and daddy was, "Who will be next? Will it be my mother, my husband, my children, or will it be me?" These "fears of death" robbed me of the peace God wanted to give me.

...When a member of my family was late in arriving home, I feared they had had an accident or been kidnapped.

...When the children ran a fever, I feared a dread disease.

...When they got a severe stomachache, I feared my cooking had given them food poisoning.

...When we flew in an airplane, I feared it would crash.

...When I drove a car, I feared I might hit someone.

Death seemed to be the end result of all my fears because death meant "separation" to me and I could not bear the thought of losing another loved one. However, living in a constant state of apprehension plays havoc with our adrenal system and can make us very sick—physically as well as emotionally. Unless I could find a healthy release for my fears, peace would evade me forever.

That's when Philippians 4:6, 7 came into my life:

> Don't *worry* about anything.
> Instead *pray* about everything.

Our whole family knows this verse by heart now and we repeat it to one another whenever one of us slips into an unhealthy "worrywart" pattern. We are breaking old habits (of worry) and establishing new habits (of praying).

...Each morning I pray with every member of our family before they go off to work and school. We place each other in God's care!

...After breakfast, I kneel down with my "prayer book." It is filled with pictures of my loved ones. I thank God for taking care of them during the day and I lift their individual needs before his throne of grace.

...Whenever someone is late in getting home or we're having a particular family problem, I often go to our living room worship center for special prayers.

...At the dinner table we take hands and thank God for watching over us and blessing our day.

...At bedtime we commit our family into God's protecting hands.

Does this mean that every member of our family is safe and secure from all harm? Yes, as far as God is concerned, it does. He is watching over us whether we live or die and he will continue to take care of us whether we live on earth or in heaven. This is the kind of peace that truly passes all understanding!

THANKING GOD BRINGS PEACE

It is not always easy to "thank God in all things," but the Scriptures tell us to do this.

> Always be joyful. Always keep on praying. No matter what happens, always be thankful, for this is God's will for you who belong to Christ Jesus (1 Thess. 5:16-18].

Some people insist this means we are supposed to praise God for:

...a divorce.
...the death of a loved one.
...a runaway child.
...a personal assault.
...a loss of a job.
...a bankruptcy, etc.

But I am quite convinced that the heavenly Father wants no praise for these kinds of situations. For God is the source of all good—not the source of evil. However, I do believe that the Father wants us to praise him *while* we are walking through our "valleys of death and despair."

Whenever our family has undergone a "trial by fire," we have learned through experience that "*praise* and *thanksgiving*" are the best way to regain our equilibrium. When we've been filled with deep distress,

...ridiculed,
...denied,
...betrayed, or
...mistreated,

we can respond like Jesus did: "Father, forgive these people, for they don't know what they are doing" (Luke 23:34).

Brother Paul has some good advice, too:

> We patiently endure suffering and hardships and trials of every kind. . . . We stand true to the Lord whether

> others honor us or despise us, whether they criticize or command us . . . . The world ignores us but we are known to God; . . . Our hearts ache but at the same time we have the joy of the Lord! [2 Cor. 6:5, 8-10].

Is it possible, with the Holy Spirit living inside of us, that we can do the same? Can we really do what Paul suggests?

> Never pay back evil for evil. Do things in such a way that everyone can see you are honest clear through. Don't quarrel with anyone. Be at *peace* with everyone just as much as possible [Rom. 12:17, 18].

Yes, we can, because the same resurrection power we read about in the New Testament is also available today. We, too, can turn an enemy into a friend by giving them a double and triple dose of God's love, God's joy, and God's peace. Start today! Melt somebody with your tender loving care. Watch God perform a miracle before your very eyes.

When people hurt us,
  laugh at us,
  make fun of us,
  lie about us,
  criticize us,
  put us down,
  intimidate us;
let's respond with a forgiving spirit,
  a loving heart,
  a cheerful disposition,
  a happy smile,
  a warm greeting, and
  a bushelful of good, positive prayers.

I can promise you from personal experience that you will receive a victory in Christ. When you start *praising* and *thanking* God for the person who has hurt you, a *peace* will flood your soul that passes all understanding!

TRUSTING JESUS BRINGS PEACE

If *praying* and *thanking* God bring peace—wait until you try *trusting*! I am convinced that when Jesus said we must "become as little children to enter the Kingdom of Heaven"

(Matt. 18:3), he was talking about *trust*. If you want to draw close to the heart of God, trust him more and more and more every day!

> Just as you *trusted* Christ to save you, *trust* him, too, for each day's problems; live in vital union with him. Let your roots grow down into him and draw up nourishment from him. See that you go on growing in the Lord and become strong and vigorous in the truth you were taught. Let your lives overflow with joy and thanksgiving for all he has done [Col. 2:6, 7].

Where do you need to trust Christ? What areas of peace are lacking in your life?

I used to be frightened of people.
At school and office parties, I often "hid in the restroom," because I didn't know what to say. But God has taught me in his Word to "comfort those who are frightened; take tender care of those who are weak; and be patient with everyone" (1 Thess. 5:14). Now I reach out to others and forget about myself. *Oh, what peace!*

I used to fear getting up to speak.
I never raised my hand in class even when I knew the answer. But God has taught me in his Word, "How shall they ask him to save them unless they believe in him? And how can they believe in him if they have never heard about him? And how can they hear about him unless someone tells them?" (Rom. 10:14). Now I've asked the Lord to let me teach and write about him as long as I live. *Oh, what peace!*

I used to wake up with "anxiety attacks"
and think I was dying.
I would wake my husband out of a sound sleep and ask him to pray for me. But God has taught me in his Word, "Don't be afraid, for I have ransomed you; I have called you by name; you are mine. When you go through deep waters and great trouble, I will be with you. When you go through rivers of difficulty, you will not drown! When you walk through the fire of oppression, you will not be burned up—the flames will

not consume you. For I am the Lord your God, your Savior" (Isa. 43:1-3). Now I trust him to see me through my trials and tribulations. I repeat his promises aloud in the midst of my troubles. *Oh, what peace!*

I used to worry about growing old.
I pulled out my first gray hairs and checked with the doctors every time I got a new ache or pain. But God has taught me in his Word, "I have created you and cared for you since you were born. I will be your God through all your lifetime; yes, even when your hair is white with age. I made you and I will care for you. I will carry you along and be your Savior" (Isa. 46:3, 4). Now I can smile at my wrinkles and gray hair and say, "Thanks, God." *Oh, what peace!*

God is still working on me in other areas. He's teaching me about peace:

...in my driving on the freeways;
...in my flying all over the world;
...in raising our "second family" of teenagers;
...in being a good mother-in-law and grandma;
...in writing books and putting together radio and TV programs;
...in my bouts with illness and pain;
...in my acceptance of change.

I expect to go on learning about God's peace for the rest of my life. But the minute you or I sense a "need for peace" in any area of our lives, we must remember to:

Pray about everything;
Thank God for his answers; and,
Trust Christ to keep our thoughts and hearts quiet and at rest.

Let's find a "retreat center" in our homes where we can go whenever family life gets "uptight." Let's stay alone with our Lord until he relieves our tensions and refills us with his peace. We won't come out to face the family until the Master Peacemaker has done his healing work in our heart and mind.

When you and I do this we will experience God's peace which is more wonderful than the human mind can understand.

THE FRUIT OF PEACE

Peace, like love and joy, is a *gift from God.* So ask Jesus to fill you with the fruit of his Holy Spirit. Then you can know his peace and let it overflow onto others.

FOUR
Taste the Fruit of PATIENCE

Take time to laugh and sing and play, and cuddle them a bit.
Tell them a story now and then, and steal a little time to sit.
And listen to their childish talk, or take them for a little walk.

You do not know it now, but soon they will be gone . . . the years are swift.
For life just marches on and on, and Heaven holds no sweeter gift
Than a small boy with tousled hair who leaves his toys just anywhere.

Take time to hear their prayers at night. To really cherish and enjoy
A little girl with flaxen curls, and the wonder of a boy . . .
They ask so little when they're small, just love and tenderness . . . that's all. (*Vermont Home Guards*)

These precious words are on the front page of my Picture Prayer Book. I can refer to them daily while looking at a snapshot of our family walking on the beach. It reminds me of how fast our children grow up. Praise God, we have an eleven-year span between our first two and last two, so we have been able to "laugh, sing, play, cuddle, tell stories, take walks, and say prayers" for a long, long time now. I found this poem in a Holt Orphanage Newspaper, so it was very appropriate when our adopted Korean daughter presented me with a watercolor poster that read:

> I love my mom because she tucks me in bed all the time. She kisses me "good night." Molly

Tucking in bed was a tradition we started when I returned from the sanitarium at age twenty-seven . . . a song-time, talk-time, and prayer-time. These nighttime and morning moments in bed mean a great deal to our children. Recently I came across another note written by our eldest many years ago:

> I love you Mother. I hope you have a happy Mother's Day. I would like you to have a treat in the morning. (No guesses.) You never forget to care for me and give me my breakfast and you wake me up in a nice mood.
> Love, Jeff

What a privilege it is to be a parent! God has given us the opportunity to participate with him in the raising of our children. Listen to his instructions back in the days of Moses.

> O Israel, listen: Jehovah is our God, Jehovah alone. You must love him with all your heart, soul, and might. And you must think constantly about these commandments I am giving you today. You must *teach* them to your children and talk about these commandments when you are at home or out for a walk; at bedtime and the first thing in the morning [Deut. 6:4-7].

Jesus often quoted portions of this Scripture in his teachings and when it came time for him to leave this earth, he commissioned his followers to:

> Go and make disciples in all nations, baptizing them into the name of the Father and of the Son and of the Holy Spirit, and then *teach* these new disciples to obey all the commands I have given you; and be sure of this—I am with you always, even to the end of the world! [Matt. 28:19, 20].

There we have it, in both the Old and New Testaments, we are expected to *teach* and *disciple* those within our keeping. Our Lord Jesus promises to be with us all the way. It won't always be easy. We'll need plenty of *patience*. But God will supply our every need. Let's look at several situations where the "*fruit of patience*" is of prime importance!

PATIENCE IN RAISING CHILDREN

Are you impatient with immaturity?
...When the baby throws up on your party clothes?
...When your toddler spills his milk at every other meal?
...When your preschooler wets his pants?
...When your grade schooler loses his bike?
...When your Jr. Higher gets caught playing hooky?
...When your Sr. Higher bangs up the car?

Ask any parent for a blow-by-blow description of the ups and downs of raising children and you will fill volumes. Many volumes have been written on how to "bring up" a child. They vary from decade to decade.

Some say, "Put them on a schedule."
Others say, "Feed them when they're hungry."
"Be permissive!" . . . "Be strict!"
"Spank!" . . . "Reason!"
"Give rewards!" . . . "Put them on restrictions!"
"Allowances are OK!" . . . "No pay!"

So what's a parent to do? Having raised children in the fifties, sixties, and seventies, we have been exposed to a variety of "suggestions" and "advice." Some we've even "invented" on our own.

But the best book we've found on child psychology is God's Book. From Genesis to Revelation its pages are filled with wise counsel and personal examples. The most often quoted "advice to parents" is found in the Old Testament book of Proverbs:

> *Teach* a child to *choose* the *right* path, and when he is *older* he will *remain* upon it [Prov. 22:6].

Notice, it doesn't say, "*Make* the child"; it says, "*Teach* a child," so he can "choose the right path." There's a big difference! God's whole plan of salvation is set upon the premise of "free will." Jesus came to *teach* us how to *choose* the *right path*. The decision is up to us! Over and over again in the Bible we see examples of those who chose the right path and those who chose the wrong path (even in the same families).

Abel chose God's way—Cain chose his own way.
Jacob chose God's way—Esau chose his own way.
Joseph chose God's way—his brothers chose their own way.
David chose God's way—Saul chose his own way.
Peter chose God's way—Judas chose his own way.

All of these men had been taught by their fathers and forefathers how to live; but some ignored their faith and chose to do their own thing. Their parents knew the frustrations of disobedient children and they often reaped the results from generation to generation.

It's no different today. We as parents do the best we can with the wisdom and understanding we have. We sure can't take full credit for all the good results and we must not take full blame for all the bad results. We can only set the stage and pray. Our children must "play their own parts" on life's stage. They will reap the blessings and consequences of their own behavior and choices.

But *patience* on our part plays an important role in "setting the stage." Listen to Brothers Paul and Peter:

> And now a word to you parents. Don't keep on *scolding* and *nagging* your children, making them *angry* and *resentful*. Rather bring them up with the *loving discipline* the Lord himself approves with *suggestions* and *godly advice* [Eph. 6:4].
>
> You should be like *one big happy family*, full of sympathy toward each other, *loving* one another with *tender hearts* and *humble minds*. Don't repay evil for evil. Don't snap back at those who say unkind things about you. Instead, *pray* for God's help for them, for we are to be *kind* to others and God will *bless* us for it [1 Pet. 3:8, 9].

These golden nuggets of truth can be applied in our families with amazing results. We know from thirty years of experience!

We've made the mistake of scolding and nagging our children to the point of making them angry and resentful—

and we all suffered in the process. *But* we've found we can get much better results when our discipline is loving—filled with suggestions and godly advice. (Read Hebrews 12:1-15.)

We've made the mistake of snapping back at our children when they were in a bad mood—letting their mood determine our mood. *But* we've found we can get much better results when we pray for God's help—loving each other with tender hearts and humble minds. (Read 1 Corinthians 13 over and over again.)

It's a fine line we parents walk! But, remember "impatience with immaturity" can be one of our greatest enemies. It can keep us from "enjoying" our children at every age.

This does not mean we throw discipline out the window and let the child do whatever he wants. (God forbid!) We still have our "family rules" with their "built-in consequences"—just like God does for his family. The Father has his hand of mercy and his hand of justice; but like the Father we must never give up on our children. By cultivating a mature atmosphere of positive attitudes and spiritual values, we can help our children discover God's way. When we follow it ourselves, we "set the stage" for them to *choose* the right path. So:

...Encourage them when they make wise choices.
...Pick them up when they make wrong choices.

Read through Proverbs every month—(one chapter per day). Review Paul and Peter's pointers on family life in Ephesians 6 and 1 Peter 3. Study Romans 12 and Hebrews 12. Put each new insight into practice. Repeat it over and over again until it becomes a "holy habit."

PATIENCE WITH LIFE'S INCONSISTENCIES

Do you get mad at the "bad guys"? You're doing the best you can to live God's way and things still go wrong, while the neighbor down the street goes merrily on his way with no apparent problems. "It's just not fair!" you exclaim.

...I get sick—he stays well.
...My hot water heater breaks—his doesn't.
...My car breaks down—he gets a new one.
...My kids get into trouble—his never get caught.

...I'm honest on my income tax—he cheats.
...I keep my dog off his lawn—he let's his come on my lawn.
...I go to church every Sunday—he plays golf.
...I tithe—he buys another possession.
"Where are my blessings?" you cry.

God's "kids" are richly blessed with "surprise serendipities" every day. If you haven't discovered this, then you are letting impatience rob you of your inheritance. The Psalmist knew the secret of "godly patience" when he wrote:

> Rest in the Lord; wait *patiently* for him to act. Don't be envious of evil men who prosper. Stop your anger! Turn off your wrath. Don't fret and worry—it only leads to harm. For the wicked shall be destroyed, but those who trust the Lord shall be given every blessing [Psa. 37:7-9].

He went on to say:

> Don't be *impatient* for the Lord to act! Keep traveling steadily along his pathway and in due season he will honor you with every blessing, and you will see the wicked destroyed [Psa. 37:34].

As the Lord draws comparisons between the godly and the ungodly, we no longer see any inconsistencies in the end.

So don't be impatient for the Lord to act! Rest in the Lord and wait! Memorize the following verses from Psalm 37.

> Be delighted with the Lord. Then he will give you all your heart's desires. Commit everything you do to the Lord. Trust him to help you do it and he will [verses 4, 5].

> The steps of good men are directed by the Lord. He delights in each step they take. If they fall it isn't fatal, for the Lord holds them with his hand [verses 23, 24].

> I have been young and now I am old. And in all my years I have never seen the Lord forsake a man who loves him; nor have I seen the children of the godly go hungry. Instead, the godly are able to be generous with their gifts and loans to others, and their children are a blessing [verses 25, 26].

Start keeping a daily journal of all the *good things* that happen to you every day. Record some of the *bad things*, too, but be sure and look for a "blessing in disguise." As God's children, "all that happens to us is working for our good if we love God and are fitting into his plans" (Rom. 8:28). Brother Paul knew about this when he said:

> We are pressed on every side by troubles, *but* not crushed and broken.
> We are perplexed because we don't know why things happen as they do, *but* we don't give up and quit.
> We are hunted down, *but* God never abandons us.
> We get knocked down, *but* we get up again and keep going [2 Cor. 4:8, 9].

Let me share with you a few entries from my daily journal (recorded at age fifty):

"Good Things"	*"Blessings in Disguise"*
1. My class sent me a dozen roses, cake, and cards for my fiftieth birthday.	I had to stand in line an hour at Motor Vehicle Division *but* got a 100 percent on my driver's test.
2. My husband took our family to see "I Do, I Do" for a celebration.	Our underground plumbing broke down for three days (no showers, no toilets, no dishwasher, etc.), *but* our neighbors came to the rescue. Repair costs were $1000, *but* the builders were at fault.
3. Our middle son is getting married and returning to an Air Force Base in the States.	The carpets were water damaged in the process, *but* I got a chance to witness to the repairmen again.

I have a close friend who recently went to the mountains with her children and grandchildren. The snow was so high they couldn't reach their cabin, so they stayed in a motel. When another storm was predicted, they feared getting "snowed in" and so returned home the next day. My friend was visibly disappointed after all their effort to get there. Her twelve-year-old grandson sensed this and said, "Grandma, God always knows what's best for us." The next day when my friend read about people getting stranded, she commented to her grandson, "It sure was good we returned or your daddy and mother wouldn't have gotten back to work on time." He smiled and repeated, "Why, of course, Grandma, God knows best." What a profound insight for a twelve-year-old.

Keep your ledger, but learn how to say, "God knows best!" When you're God's child, all of life can be a blessing if you let it. Be *patient* and wait for the "surprises" up ahead. It all balances out in the end. In fact you'll come out ahead. Trust God to work out all the details and hang in there. Patience brings rewards for the godly.

> Let us not get tired of doing what is right, for after a while we will reap a harvest of blessing if we don't get discouraged and give up [Gal. 6:9].

PATIENCE IN OUR LIMITATIONS

Have you ever had the wind knocked out of your sails? You were going along full speed ahead and out of the blue you got sick, or broke your wrist, or sprained your foot, or had surgery, or strained your back and ended up in bed, flat on your back, with nothing to do but wait—wait—wait.

This happens to all of us from time to time (even the good guys). The same bug bites us both because we live in a world that is contaminated with sin and disease and death. The Bible says:

> All creation is waiting patiently and hopefully for that future day . . . when thorns and thistles, sin, death, and decay . . . will all disappear. . . . Even we Christians, although we have the Holy Spirit within us as a foretaste of future glory, also groan to be released from pain and suffering. We, too, wait for . . . the new bodies he has promised us—bodies that will never be sick again and never die (Rom. 8:19-23).

But while we're waiting for this release, the Scriptures encourage us with these words:

> They that wait upon the Lord shall renew their strength. They shall mount up with wings like eagles. They shall run and not be weary; they shall walk and not faint (Isa. 40:31).

Do you believe this? I do! I can think of so many people who are living examples of this verse. Some may not be able to run and walk physically (people like Joni Erickson and Tara Nason), but their spirits "mount up with wings like eagles" and they are an inspiration to the people around them. They renew our strength just to watch them. If you haven't read the four books about Joni and Tara, get hold of them in your bookstore and read what happens to people who wait patiently on the Lord!

How do *you* "wait on the Lord" when you're down in bed?
...Do you spend more time reading his Word?
...Do you talk with the Father?
...Do you put a stack of hymns on your record player?
...Do you write cards and notes to other shut-ins?
...Do you read good Christian books and magazines?
...Do you pray for others who are sick?
...Do you tune in an uplifting radio or TV program?

Do you know some people who are *patient* in their limitations? Earlier I mentioned Joni and Tara, but I know many others.

My girlfriend Carol, who typed this manuscript, has a ten-year-old son who has been confined to the floor or a corrective chair all his life, *but* that doesn't hold Scotty down. He can laugh and tease and compliment you all in one breath. He gave the flag salute at the "Special Olympics" and entered some of the competition. He takes part in his school programs and loves to go on outings with his class. Scotty has blessed his family and friends with his happy spirit. He is playing here at my feet with his truck while I write this paragraph.

My own mother has suffered with rheumatoid arthritis and blood pressure problems for nearly forty years but she is known for her warm smile and happy attitude wherever she lives. She keeps busy with her projects—gardening, researching and writing our own family's version of *Roots*. Often she takes her cane and walks over to the hospital to cheer up a sick friend.

Since our real fathers and grandpas are already with Jesus, we have "adopted" other grandpas. One is a "ninety-year-old wonder." Even though he often needs to lean on us to walk the bumpy paths, he still swims several times a week at his Leisure World pool. He needs a secretary to keep up with his heavy correspondence. As a retired lawyer, he still helps family and friends with their many personal business and financial problems. He helped us adopt our little Korean daughter and he has counseled with her in the area of "memory healing." His church uses him as a witness and enabler at their retreats.

Another one of our "adopted" grandpas has worn an artificial leg for almost seventy years (he's eighty-five now) but that didn't stop him from hiking several miles to and from his church to volunteer his services in the mail room. A heart attack and recent stroke have diminished his strength *but* he still writes warm letters to his friends and family—filled with Scripture promises. His letters are the kind you save and cherish.

Upon several occasions I have sent the following Scripture to our precious senior citizens,

> Take a new grip with your tired hands, stand firm on your shaky legs, and mark out a straight, smooth path for your feet so that those who follow you, though weak and lame, will not fall and hurt themselves, but become strong [Heb. 12:12, 13].

I remind them that there are a lot of folks where they live who look to them for inspiration. God says his power shows up best in weak people, because then he can shine through them.

PATIENCE WITH PEOPLE

How are you in the "tender loving care" department? What about lazy people, frightened people, those who are emotionally, spiritually, or morally weak?

The Scriptures have some profound and power-packed advice for us to follow:

> Dear brothers, warn those who are lazy; comfort those who are frightened; take tender care of those who are weak; and be patient with everyone [1 Thess. 5:14].

Obviously God wants us to exercise *patience* and tender loving care with others.

He tells us to *warn the lazy* (not scold, just warn). In Paul's day he was writing to a group of believers who stopped working to wait for Jesus' return, expecting others to support their needs. Now this is not the Christian way, Paul says. We must all do our part in "rowing the boat."

This is especially good advice for the parent. We are never doing our children a "favor" when we allow their laziness. Regular chores are as important today as they were in the olden days (maybe even more so, in order to keep them out of twentieth century mischief). All our sons have had jobs before they were sixteen (with a school work permit), and each of them agrees this was part of their "education" in learning how to stick with a job and do it responsibly. They also appreciated the opportunity to learn how to handle their finances at a young age. So, it's our job to "warn against laziness" and provide challenging outlets.

He tells us to *comfort the frightened*—not make fun of them or laugh at their phobias. Do you sometimes get impatient with people who are easily frightened? Do you want to scold them and tell them to "grow up?"

...As a little girl I can remember crying in the night with a high fever, bad earaches, or asthma attacks. I was sometimes afraid I was dying. My parents always comforted me and soothed my fears.

...As a young bride I was frightened and cried on my wedding night so my husband of four hours had to forget himself and comfort me in his arms.

...As a middle-ager I have been frightened to drive the freeways, but my friends keep encouraging me. Even when I cried in an on-ramp lane (unable to cut into heavy traffic), my sixteen-year-old son comforted and calmed me down.

What patient people God has surrounded me with during my lifetime. Someday I'm going to write a book of praise to God for all the patient people who have helped me overcome my fears.

He tells us to *take tender care of the weak*. Is this easy for you to do? If it's a little baby, a handicapped child, a sick patient, or an elderly person, you probably don't have any trouble expressing TLC; but what about the emotionally, spiritually, and morally weak? Do you have trouble with them? This Scripture goes on to say, "Be patient with everyone."

...For those who are emotionally strong, it is sometimes hard to be patient with those who are emotionally weak.

...For those who are spiritually strong, it is sometimes hard to be patient with those who are spiritually immature.

...For those who are morally strong, it is often very difficult to be nonjudgmental of those who are morally weak.

Because of my own struggles I have little trouble identifying with the emotionally and spiritually weak people, but I have had to learn to express TLC to the morally weak. God has been teaching me how:

Through the Scriptures.
The woman at the well, the woman caught in adultery, and the realization that sin is sin, no matter what commandment you break.

Through my reading in psychology.
Learning that people's "values" have gotten mixed up along the way so that they form poor "behavioral responses" (for many complicated reasons).

Through my actual encounters with people who are struggling with moral weakness.
I have come to love them for the good qualities God has put inside them and I pray for God's "living water" to flood their lives the same way it did for the people in Scripture.

Yes, the Lord asks us to be patient with everybody—no matter what their weakness. See how patient our Father is with us.

> Even when we are too weak to have any faith left, he remains faithful to us and will help us, for he cannot disown us who are part of himself, and he will always carry out his promises to us [2 Tim. 2:13].

PATIENCE IN THE ROUGH TIMES OF LIFE

This is the real test! This is when we can grow "better" or "bitter." The choice is up to us! What do the rough times of life have to teach us? Brothers Paul and James share with us from out of their own personal experience.

> We can rejoice, too, when we run into problems and trials for we know that they are good for us—they help us learn to be patient. And patience develops strength of character in us, and helps us trust God more each time we use it until finally our hope and faith are strong and steady. Then, when that happens, we are able to hold our heads high no matter what happens and know that all is well, for we know how dearly God loves us, and we feel this warm love everywhere within us because God has given us the Holy Spirit to fill our hearts with his love [Rom. 5:3-5].

> When the way is rough, your patience has a chance to grow. So let it grow, and don't try to squirm out of your problems. For when your patience is finally in full bloom, then you will be ready for anything, strong in character, full and complete [Jas. 1:2-4].

Do those sound like goals you might want to strive for and accomplish? Or would you rather not even ask for the "gift of patience" for fear you might have to undergo a rigorous training program? Well, ask or not, these lessons are built into the warp and woof of life itself. There's no way you or I can skip the "school of hard knocks." But we can react in two ways: We can let life's rough experiences *make* us or *break* us. The choice is up to us!

The sooner we form the habit of reacting positively and patiently rather than negatively and impatiently to life's "surprises," the easier will be our walk through this earthly life.

This reminds me of the Scripture, "I can do everything God asks me to with the help of Christ who gives me the strength and power" (Phil. 4:13).

The more we believe this and the more we put it into practice, the more it will become a permanent part of our personalities. Philippians 4:13 is probably the verse I've

used more than any other verse in the Bible. It's a promise I have claimed over and over again:
...when final exams were being taken
...when my babies were being born
...before and after surgery
...when loved ones passed away
...when I have to speak
...when I need to fly
...when I'm in pain
...when I have to face a difficult challenge
...when I undertake a new assignment.

I'll have to admit that I am aware of a change taking place in my character. Each time we pass through a rough ordeal and come out victorious on the other side, it becomes a little easier the next time. We are piling up positive truth that our Lord is a "gentleman of his word." He is faithful! He never lets us down! He sticks closer than a brother!

If we want to mature into *patient people*, all we have to do is follow God's blueprint for living the Spirit-filled life:

> Do you want more and more of God's kindness and peace? Then learn to know him better and better. For as you know him better, he will give you, through his great power, everything you need for living a truly good life; he even shares his own glory and his own goodness with us! . . .
>
> You need more than faith; you must also work hard to be good. . . . then you must learn to know God better and discover what he wants you to do. Next, learn to put aside your own desire so that you will become *patient* and godly, gladly letting God have his way with you.
>
> This will make possible the next step which is for you to enjoy other people and to like them, and finally you will grow to love them deeply. The more you go on in this way, the more you will grow strong spiritually and become fruitful and useful to our Lord Jesus Christ. . . .
>
> Work hard to prove that you really are among those God has called and chosen, and then you will never stumble or fall away. And God will open wide the gates

> of heaven for you to enter into the eternal kingdom of our Lord and Savior Jesus Christ [2 Pet. 1:2-11].

The gift of patience is sculpted out of our daily living—with our children, with life's inconsistencies, with our limitations, with people, and in those rough times that come to all of us. If we yield our lives to the Master, he will work out the details.

Ask Jesus to fill you with the fruit of his Holy Spirit so you can put *his patience* into action and let it overflow onto others.

FIVE
Taste the Fruit of KINDNESS

"I will be faithful to you and honest with you.
I will share my life with you.
I will open myself to you.
I will share my innermost being with you.
I will feel your feelings with you as you feel my feelings with me.
I will accept you as you are, as God accepts both of us as we are.
I will forgive you as both of us are forgiven by God's grace.
I will seek to respond to the inspiration which you give.
I will seek to bring you inspiration, as God gives hope to both of us.
I will enter into the promises of growth with you,
That we may become one in him whose love we share
And by whose grace we live.
I will enter with you into the unfolding miracle of God's redemptive love in our lives,
Through all the days we shall share by God's grace.
My ability to give myself is not perfect now.
But I will grow in my ability to give.
Until my gift is continuous and whole."

(Royce and Karen Calhoun)

KINDNESS BEGINS WITH GIVING

Holding hands and looking into one another's eyes, my husband and I expressed these words to one another at the close of our Christian Marriage Encounter weekend. Marriage Encounter is for couples of all ages who have a good marriage but want an even closer one. This crash course in communication has grown out of our Judeo-Christian heritage. It is God's answer to the divorce dilemma.

Because Marriage Encounter must be experienced in order to be appreciated and understood, I will not go into detail about what happens—other than to say, you are given a "communication tool" that is guaranteed to work if you work it. In forty-eight hours you learn how "to walk in each other's shoes," as you open up your hearts to one another on a deeper level than you ever dreamed possible. If I were to describe how I felt on our weekend I would have to say,

I felt giddy as I did during our courtship days!
I felt elated as I did during our honeymoon!
I felt exhausted as I did during labor!
I felt fulfilled as I did after the birth of our three sons!

It was a sincere and genuine "mutual admiration" encounter with the man I married twenty-eight years ago, because we were in a climate where the Holy Spirit within us, expressed *kindness* to one another. *Kindness* is a "precious gift." It makes the giver, as well as the receiver feel like a very important person—a special child of the King.

But kindness doesn't just happen by accident. It has to be worked at, nourished, and encouraged. Think about all the attributes that originally attracted you to the persons you love. Write them down and share them with those persons. I had fun reminiscing over those attributes that first attracted me to my "Prince Charming."

1. He was the most handsome, curly-headed boy I had ever seen!
2. He had an exciting way with words that captivated my heart.
3. He made me feel warm and important and cared for whenever he was near me.
4. He was a good friend and fun to go on dates with.

5. He fixed me anything I wanted for breakfast when he was the cook at the dorm where I lived.

6. He waited patiently for me after dance and play rehearsals and seemed genuinely interested and proud of what I was doing.

7. He had nice parents and he was good and respectful to them.

8. He had a charming hometown and I loved it when he took me there.

9. His sense of humor and practical solutions gave me peace and security.

10. His physical touch caused things to happen inside of me that have never happened with any other boy.

11. His love letters and cards (whenever we were separated) sent goose bumps all over me.

12. His *kindness* and thoughtfulness in helping me with my projects gave me self-confidence.

I wondered if my husband still found me as "captivating" as when we first met. Had I "improved with age" . . . in spite of all my mistakes and hang-ups? His list set my heart to rejoicing.

1. You're a fun person to be around (both intellectually and physically stimulating).

2. You're very creative and always full of exciting ideas and thoughts.

3. You maintain a warm, loving, and beautiful home.

4. I always look forward to coming home and being with you.

5. You're fun to talk to.

6. You're a great listener.

7. You're a great friend, wife, and mother.

8. Doing things together (even simple things like a walk on the beach) is great fun with you.

9. My dreams and visions take on a new excitement when I can share them with you.

10. I want to help you fulfill some of your dreams, too.

11. I love you very much—even more than when I first met and fell in love with you.

12. I look at you as my "blood sister" (not like the Indians,

but rather because of the blood of Christ.)

13. When I think of all the good things that have happened and then I think about the future—you can quickly see why you are front and center—the top of the dream; the heart of the vision.

Beauty (physical and spiritual) is truly in the eyes of the beholder! Neither one of us is as "perfect" as these lists might sound. But we have discovered something deeper than the "storybook marriage" I had always fantasized about. We have discovered that friendship and companionship—sharing and caring—are what living together is all about. God created people because he was lonely for companionship and God created Eve because Adam needed a friend as well as a helper and lover. There is no deeper joy in marriage than being friends with your sweetheart.

King Solomon knew this when he made some of his classic comments about the marriage relationship:

> Let your manhood be a blessing; rejoice in the wife of your youth. Let her charms and tender embrace satisfy you. Let her love alone fill you with delight [Prov. 5:18, 19].
>
> If you can find a truly good wife, she is worth more than precious gems! Her husband can trust her, and she will richly satisfy his needs. She will not hinder him, but help him all her life [Prov. 31:10-12].

As we look further into that "kindly woman" of Proverbs 31, we see other traits that endear her to her family. Not only is she worth more than precious gems and not only does she satisfy her husband's needs, but she is also:

...a good homemaker
...a career woman
...a bargain shopper
...a hard worker
...a woman who sews for the poor
...a woman who sews for her family
...a woman of strength and dignity
...a woman who has no fear of old age
...a woman whose words are wise
...a woman for whom *kindness* is the rule

...one who is never lazy
...one who reverences God.

As a result, her children bless her, her husband praises her, and the leaders of nations honor her. All this wins her the "Best Wife of the Year" trophy when her husband exclaims:

> There are many fine women in the world, but you are the best of them all [Prov. 31:29].

What a tribute!

Does the "man of the house" get equal time in the Scriptures? He sure does! Listen to these descriptions of his "kindly qualities":

> Where is the man who fears the Lord? God will teach him how to choose the best. He shall live within God's circle of blessing, and his children shall inherit the earth. Friendship with God is reserved for those who reverence him. With them alone he shares the secrets of his promises [Psa. 5:12-14].
>
> Blessings on all who reverence and trust the Lord—on all who obey him! Their reward shall be prosperity and happiness. Your wife shall be contented in your home. And look at all those children! There they sit around the dinner table as vigorous and healthy as young olive trees. That is God's reward to those who reverence and trust him. May the Lord continually bless you with heaven's blessings as well as with human joys. May you live to enjoy your grandchildren! [Psa. 128:1-6].

Those last verses remind me of our expanding family sitting around the table for Thanksgiving, Christmas, and birthday celebrations. No wonder God created homes and families. They're a very integral and necessary "haven for growth" while here on Planet Earth—getting us ready for our heavenly homes. *Kindness* is learned in the family—living together, working together, and playing together.

At the end of our summer vacation overseas, our Air Force son (who is stationed in England) put us on a train headed for the airport and our return flight to the states. A couple of weeks later this touching letter arrived.

> What a truly sad day Saturday was as we said our good-byes at Victoria Train Station in London. My

> eyes became watery as I made my lonely walk back to the car. . . . Saying good-bye to loved ones is not easy! Driving home I went back in my mind over and over all the wonderful things we did together—memories I'm sure we'll remember forever. Our time together as a family—talking, laughing, sharing our love and happiness meant so much. I love you all very much and thank God for the many blessings he gave us.

KINDNESS BEGETS BLESSINGS

As we said in an earlier chapter, God is so *kind* to "his kids!" I encouraged you to keep a daily journal recording all of God's surprises. How have you been doing? While our family was together for four weeks, I recorded over 100 of God's "serendipities" in my travel journal. What a joy it is to reread and relive these memories.

"Thank You, Lord, for Being So Kind"

1. For breakfast together at 2:00 AM on the morning of our arrival.
2. For making it possible for all seven of us to stay together in our son's cozy 200-year-old, two-story, two-bedroom, one-bath village home.
3. For waking us up to a praise album on the stereo.
4. For our morning stroll past flower gardens to a 500-year-old church.
5. For a borrowed van to tour the countryside.
6. For our fourteen-year-old's prayers over pizza at an English pub.
7. For a fun time of peeling potatoes with our future daughter-in-law.
8. For the joy of watching our son play with his future baby daughter.
9. For prayer time in the English abbeys and European cathedrals.
10. For empty washers at the A.F.B. to catch up on our laundry with our daughter-in-law.

11. For monkeys playing on our car hood in the wildlife reserve.

12. For nice gifts at good prices for friends back home.

13. For the plans we made to start a family "Potato Pub" back in the states.

14. For not getting lost in the tubes.

15. For not getting seasick on the Channel.

16. For lifts that didn't get stuck.

17. For a key to the hotel bathtub.

18. For "room service" in Innsbruck (Daddy bringing a breakfast tray to his little daughter).

19. For getting back down the mountain after a surprise hailstorm on top the Alps.

20. For the Austrian family who sang and danced for us.

21. For our reunion with German friends (after sixteen years apart).

22. For a private trip down the Rhine.

23. For "boat camping" on the Thames.

24. For the older boys treating the senior citizens to a "night out on the town."

25. For a house call from the vicar.

26. For two birthday parties with our future granddaughter.

27. For Sunday chapel with our son's neighbors.

28. For a safe flight home.

This is just one fourth of all the "serendipities" recorded but it will give you an idea of the simple little "kindnesses" to look for in a day. And remember, a happy mood is contagious. When you have an attitude of praise, others will pick up the habit. Our whole busload of foreign travelers caught the "spirit of kindness." We laughed, sang, and clapped our way across Europe. Our goal had been to bring Christ's love wherever we went and thanks to the Holy Spirit, this was accomplished.

> I will praise you everywhere around the world, in every nation. For your loving kindness is great beyond measure, high as the heavens. Your faithfulness reaches the skies [Psa. 108:3, 4].

When fathers, mothers, children, and young people respond to God's kindness with praise, they spread God's blessings to others.

KINDNESS BREAKS DOWN BARRIERS

Kindness begins with God—moves into our homes and then spreads throughout the world. Kindness is not just for relatives and friends; it's also for strangers and even enemies.

> There is a saying, "Love your *friends* and hate your enemies." But I say: Love your *enemies*! Pray for those who *persecute* you! In that way you will be acting as true sons of your Father in heaven. For he gives his sunlight to both the evil and the good, and sends rain on the just and on the unjust too. . . . If you are friendly only to your friends, how are you different from anyone else? Even the heathen do that [Matt. 5:43-47].

The Bible is full of stories that show kindness to strangers and across racial barriers. One of the most precious examples is found in the Old Testament in the book of Ruth. One of the verses has been immortalized in song.

> I want to go wherever you go, and to live wherever you live; your people shall be my people, and your God shall be my God [Ruth 1:16].

These words came from the lips of a young Moabite widow named Ruth. They were spoken to her Hebrew mother-in-law, Naomi. This touching scene occurred when Naomi decided to return to her homeland in Bethlehem. She, too, was a recent widow. Her husband and two sons had died while they were living in Moab. They had moved to this pagan land during a time of famine in their land. Their Jewish sons had married Gentile girls. They would not be well accepted back in Naomi's hometown, so their mother-in-law encouraged them to stay in Moab and remarry. Orpha chose to stay but Ruth chose to go with her mother-in-law. This was a very kind thing to do, but no doubt Naomi's kindness to Ruth prompted her response. She wanted to live with Naomi's people and she wanted to worship their God.

As we said earlier, "Kindness begets kindness," and in a very short time Ruth's kindness was noticed by a handsome Hebrew relative named Boaz. He was destined to become her "kinsman redeemer" (a Jewish tradition whereby the relative of the widow helps rescue the paternal estate and carry on the family name). In Ruth, chapters 2 and 3, we discover a variety of ways that "kindness breaks down barriers." Let's look at a few:

1. Kindness is being warm and friendly to your employees! (2:4)
2. Kindness is noticing that somebody new has been added! (2:5)
3. Kindness is going over to meet that person! (2:8)
4. Kindness is looking after that person's welfare! (2:9)
5. Kindness is recognizing the good qualities in another! (2:11)
6. Kindness is asking God to bless others! (2:12)
7. Kindness is sharing our lunch with another person! (2:14)
8. Kindness is surprising other people! (2:16)
9. Kindness is gracious and intuitive! (3:10)
10. Kindness is conscientious and works out the details! (3:11)
11. Kindess is discreet! (3:14)
12. Kindness is generous! (3:15)

These twelve attributes of kindness apply to Boaz's response to Ruth. His actions caused Ruth and Naomi to "praise the Lord" (2:19, 20). Can you imagine what would happen in offices and neighborhoods if a newcomer was exposed to these same twelve attributes?

There's another powerful story in the New Testament that illustrates how kindness breaks down barriers. It is the well-known "Good Samaritan story."

> A Jew going on a trip from Jerusalem to Jericho was attacked by bandits. They stripped him of his clothes and money, beat him up, and left him lying half dead beside the road.
>
> By chance a Jewish priest came along; and when he saw the man lying there, he crossed to the other side of the road and passed him by. A Jewish Temple-assistant walked over and looked at him lying there, but then went on.
>
> But a despised Samaritan came along, and when he

> saw him, he felt deep pity. Kneeling beside him the Samaritan soothed his wounds with medicine and bandaged them. Then he put the man on his donkey and walked along beside him till they came to an inn, where he nursed him through the night. The next day he handed the innkeeper two twenty-dollar bills and told him to take care of the man. "If his bill runs higher than that," he said, "I'll pay the difference the next time I am here" [Luke 10:30-35].

Then Jesus sums up the whole story by challenging his questioner to "go and do the same!"

Actually you and I see something similar to this enacted on our crowded highways everyday. A car breaks down or runs out of gas—and there it sits on the shoulder of the road. Its occupants turn on the emergency lights, peer under the open hood, crawl underneath to fix a flat, or hike to the nearest phone or service station. In the meantime hundreds of cars speed by.

You, like me, have probably been in both predicaments. Sometimes you are the "victim," other times you are the "passerby."

I remember in our early married days going to a drive-in movie on the outskirts of our little village. We left our two little boys home with a sitter. About midnight we headed for home on an unlighted country trunk road. We noticed the fuel gauge on empty as the car sputterd to a halt. We got out in the pitch black night and stood by the headlights—waving and watching car after car pass us by. After what seemed like an hour, a police car stopped, picked us up, and took us into town to get a can of gas. Now I don't know how many "priests" or "pastors" or "temple assistants" passed us by, but I remember that "Samaritan policeman" looked mighty good.

Another time we were traveling through one of Southern California's thick soupy fogs, where you can't see beyond the hood of your car, when our headlights went out. So we stopped the car and turned on the inside lights in hopes nobody would hit us. Finally a fellow traveller said, "Follow my taillights"; but he zoomed off so fast we lost sight of him and sat still again until another Good Samaritan said,

"Follow me," and we drove very, very slow until he deposited us on our home street.

I think the Good Samaritan story is telling us to care enough for our fellow human beings to "get involved" even when it might mean:

...giving up some time to stop and help!

...giving up some money to meet their current need!

Modern day analogies of the Good Samaritan story are obviously not limited to "stalled cars" on the freeway. Let's look at a few more twentieth century examples:

...When someone is laid up in the hospital after surgery and you take time to go visit them, hold their hand and pray with them—you are being a Good Samaritan!

...When a little child in your neighborhood never gets to go on any outings and you include him or her in your family picnic—you are being a Good Samaritan!

...When you know someone doesn't drive and you offer to take them here and there—you are being a Good Samaritan!

...When the church puts out cries for help as Sunday school teachers, ushers, greeters, servers, counselors—and you respond—you are being a Good Samaritan!

...When you visit a prison, a nursing home, read to children in a hospital, write cards and notes to shut-ins—you are being a Good Samaritan!

...When you use every opportunity you can to share Christ's love with the people God sends into your home—you are being a Good Samaritan!

...When you share your possessions (house, car, food, clothes, and money) with people in need—you are being a Good Samaritan!

Being a Good Samaritan simply means being willing to get involved in God's heartaches here on Planet Earth . . . bringing a little kindness to others. As Jesus said:

> I was hungry and you fed me; I was thirsty and you gave me water; I was a stranger and you invited me into your homes; naked and you clothed me; sick and in prison and you visited me [Matt. 25:35-46].

Yes, when we are *kind* to those in need, we are showing *kindness* to Christ!

KINDNESS BUILDS BRIDGES

If kindness can break down barriers, it can also build bridges—between parent and child—between brother and brother. Once again the Scriptures are full of good illustrations. Two of the most famous examples are found in Genesis 45 and Luke 15.

Joseph builds bridges with his brothers.

> Joseph could stand it no longer . . . He wept aloud. His sobs could be heard throughout the palace. . . "I am Joseph!" he said to his brothers (who had sold him into Egyptian slavery years before). But his brothers couldn't say a word, they were so stunned with surprise. . . . "Don't be angry with yourselves. . . . God sent me here ahead of you to preserve your lives. . . . God has sent me here to keep you and your families alive, so that you will become a great nation. Yes, it was God who sent me here not you! . . . God turned into good what you meant for evil. . . . Don't be afraid. Indeed, I myself will take care of you and your families." And he spoke very kindly to them, reassuring them [Portions of Genesis 45, 50].

A father builds bridges with his son.

> While he was still a long distance away, his father saw him coming and was filled with loving pity and ran and embraced and kissed him.
>
> *Son:* "Father I have sinned against heaven and you and am not worthy of being called your son."
>
> *Father:* "Quick! Bring the finest robe in the house and put it on him. And a jeweled ring for his finger; and shoes! And kill the calf we have in the fattening pen. We must celebrate with a feast for this son of mine was dead and he's returned to life. He was lost and is found" [Portions of Luke 15].

In both illustrations there was a *reunion* and *celebration*. When kindness builds bridges, reconciliation takes place. Where do we need to build bridges?

Has a brother or sister "sold you down the river?" Can you say with Joseph, "God turned into good what you meant for evil." Can you say it very kindly and can you reassure them that everything is OK now, because you have truly forgiven them?

Has a son or daughter run away from home and come back, disillusioned? Can you say with the prodigal's father, "We must celebrate with a feast. He (or she) was dead and is now alive. He (or she) was lost and now is found."

I've known many families who have forgiven past hurts and opened their arms to returning loved ones. To see bitterness roll away and tears of joy return is like watching Jesus raise Lazarus out of the grave. It's a miracle!

Kindness is a delightful "fruit of the Spirit." It tastes delicious and it is very precious.

Ask Jesus to fill you with the fruit of his Holy Spirit so you can act on his kindness and let it overflow onto others.

SIX
Taste the Fruit of GOODNESS

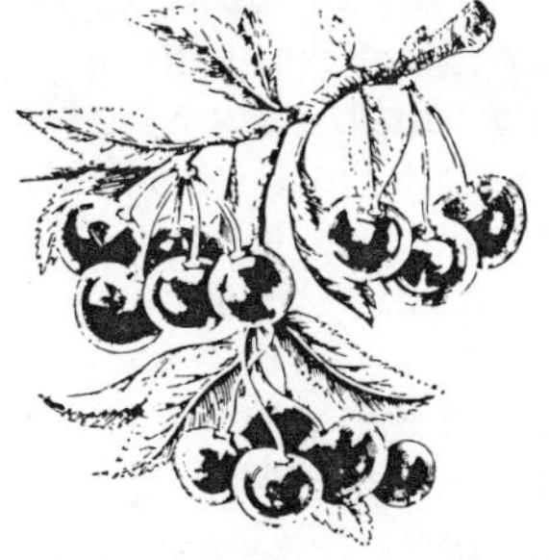

Happy are all who perfectly follow the laws of God. Happy are all who search for God, and always do his will, rejecting compromise with evil, and walking only in his paths. You have given us your laws to obey—oh, how I want to follow them consistently. Then . . . I will have a clean record. . . . Open my eyes to see wonderful things in your Word. I am but a pilgrim here on earth; how I need a map—and your commands are my chart and guide. I long for your instructions more than I can tell . . . I cling to your commands and follow them as closely as I can. Lord, don't let me make a mess of things. If you will only help me to want your will, then I will follow your laws even more closely. Just tell me what to do and I will do it, Lord. As long as I live I'll wholeheartedly obey. Make me walk along the right paths for I know how delightful they really are. . . . Now teach me good judgment as well as knowledge. For your laws are my guide. I used to wander off until you punished me; now I closely follow all you say. You are good and do only good; make me follow your lead. . . . The punishment you gave me was the best thing that could have happened to me, for it taught me to pay attention to your laws. They are more valuable to me than millions in silver and gold! . . . I know, O Lord, . . . that your punishment was right and did me good. Now let your loving kindness comfort me, just as you promised. Surround me with your tender mercies, that I may live. For your law is my delight. . . . Your words are a flashlight to light the path ahead of me, and keep me from stumbling. . . . Your laws are wonderful; no wonder I obey them. As your plan unfolds, even the simple can understand it. No wonder I wait expectantly for each of your commands. . . . I have thoroughly tested your promises and that is why I love them so much. . . . I rejoice in your laws like one who finds a great treasure. . . . Those who love your laws have great peace of heart and mind and do not stumble" [Portions of Psalm 119].

I am convinced that down deep in our hearts we long to "be good" and "stay good." We like ourselves much better when we do those things that are pleasing in God's sight. Oh, we know that God loves us even when we are bad (the same way we love our children when they misbehave), but we also know the joy that we experience when we follow God's way to the good life. Brother John describes this feeling when he writes:

> And now, my little children, stay in happy fellowship with the Lord so that when he comes you will be sure that all is well, and will not have to be ashamed and shrink back from meeting him [1 John 2:28].

When we allow God's goodness to possess us, when we are yielded to his will, and following his pathways, then we enjoy:

...a clear conscience
...an inner smile
...a warm glow and
...a winning personality.

I'll never forget a simple sermon on "goodness" given by a saint of God whose brain was so filled with cancer he could no longer recall Scripture or remember people's names. He had been an associate evangelist with the Billy Graham team for many years, but when we knew him he was the director of a family camp we attended every summer. When cancer was first discovered, he underwent surgery and chemotherapy, but the cruel disease continued to take its toll upon his body. One Thanksgiving weekend, near the end of his life, he asked to preach at our conference. We sat on the edge of our seats as our beloved friend (now thin and wasted from the cancer) walked up to the pulpit. He spoke very slowly and sincerely for about twenty minutes. The two main points of his message were:

God came to make us good and
God came to keep us good!

So simple and yet so profound. After the sermon we all filed past our great leader to kiss him goodbye and he kept repeating two phrases over and over again,

"I love you" and
"Isn't God good!"

If God's goodness could so consume this man's mind, that even cancer could not eat it away—then wouldn't you agree that God's goodness is very, very real? God is so great that we cannot fathom the wonders of his universe and yet so simple that even a person with limited mental capacity can grasp the love and goodness of the Father.

Do you need to speak to God and have God speak to you? You don't have to say a long formal prayer. Do you want to be made good and kept good? Then tell him how you feel inside—right now! Simply say,

"Jesus, this is ________________ (add your name).
Please make me good, and
please keep me good.
Thank you so much. Amen."

Because God is a good God, he will rejoice when he hears you utter this prayer from deep down in your heart. The Psalmist David once uttered this kind of prayer:

> Search me, O God, and know my heart; test my thoughts. Point out anything you find in me that makes you sad, and lead me along the path of everlasting life [Psa. 139:23, 24].

As I write this chapter today, our little girl is upstairs in her room listening to her mama's lecture tape on "goodness." I am asking her to outline what she hears—because she chose *not* to walk God's path today. There's a shortcut to her Jr. High across the railroad track. All the school children know this is "off limits," but from time to time they disobey in order to save a couple of blocks of walking. Today I happened to be driving our high school boy to school because his Moped ran out of gas en route. On the way home I happened to glance up to the railroad tracks and saw our daughter. I immediately stopped the car and went after her. Her expression when she saw me is familiar to any parent who has "caught their child in the act." I thank God for answering my morning prayers. My husband and I had taken hands to talk with the Father before beginning our day, and one of my petitions had been "Protect our children from all evil," since there is such unbelievable temptation and pressure upon our children today.

In seeking God's guidance as to how to discipline our youngest today, I felt he wanted me to give her some constructive learning experiences. Since I was doing this chapter on "goodness," it seemed logical to let her listen to the taped lesson and take notes. I've been encouraged as I read her comments. Right at the very beginning she picked out a very revealing statement.

> "Goodness is that blessed fruit of the spirit that gives us a clean conscience, an inner smile, a warm glow, and a winning personality. . . . God is a good God and he came to earth to make us good." (That's the message in a nutshell.)

Then she went on to quote David's words about "searching his heart and testing his thoughts." I'm sure our little girl was applying these words to her own behavior. In fact her whole attitude has changed and so has mine. Now we can talk rationally about why it is so important to walk God's path, instead of the "railroad" path. Just as the school has enforced this rule to protect the children from getting hurt by speeding trains, so God has set up his "laws of love" to protect us from harm. He knows what is best for us and that's why he gave us the Ten Commandments. That's also why Jesus elaborated upon these in his Sermon on the Mount.

God's Rules Are Simple. Jesus condensed them into two commandments.

1. Love the Lord your God with all your heart, soul, and mind.
2. Love your neighbor as much as you love yourself [Matt. 22:37-39].

This is the perfect order for producing goodness.

God first
Others second
Ourselves third

It is important to remember that God's goodness is based on *love* as well as *law*. As Brother Paul said: "The law *showed* me my sin." So it is good! Guilt drives us into the arms of Grace. When we learn how to live in the arms of Grace, we are freed from a life of legalism.

In the flyleaf of my Bible I have written a very thought-provoking statement explaining how "God's goodness" operates through his family:

Law makes us *act* from *outward compulsion*
whereas
Love makes us *serve* from *inward compassion.*

If "love" is God's answer to living the "good life," why do we sometimes break the rules? Why does my little girl take a shortcut across the railroad tracks? Why does our son get mad at his Moped for running out of gas? Why do I respond in agitation to their immaturity? Why don't we always make right responses and right reactions?

WHY DO WE BREAK THE RULES?

My little girl and I talked about this today. We talked about those three opponents we all face everyday:

1. Our own self-will
2. The world's pressures
3. The enemy (Satan)

But none of this is new to our generation. Back in Adam and Eve's day they encountered temptation too. They yielded to the serpent's encouragement to "eat of the forbidden tree," and ever since mankind has been living in the "fallen state." Many times we, like our first parents, choose to do what we want to do when we want to do it. And that's where all the heartache comes in. We were made to "be good" (as our conference pastor had said), and when we're not, we suffer the bitter consequences. Brother James had deep insights into all of us when he said:

> Happy is the man who doesn't . . . do wrong when he is

> tempted, for afterwards he will get as his reward the crown of life that God has promised those who love him. And remember, when someone wants to do wrong it is never God who is tempting him, for God never wants us to do wrong and never tempts anyone else to do it. Temptation is the pull of man's own evil thoughts and wishes [Jas. 1:12-14].

HOW CAN WE COMBAT OUR OPPONENTS?

When my daughter and I talked about why she had decided to take the shortcut, she admitted it was not God's idea—but her own idea. But here's where the "good news" comes in. Christians don't have to excuse their behavior anymore with the words: "I can't help it! . . . I'm only human!" We are no longer "only human." Something *new* has been added! Now we have "supernatural" help through God's Holy Spirit.

> The wrong desires that come into your life aren't anything new and different. Many others have faced exactly the same problems before. . . . No temptation is irresistible. You can trust God to keep the temptation from becoming so strong that you can't stand up against it, for he has promised this and will do what he says. He will show you how to escape temptation's power so that you can bear up patiently against it [1 Cor. 10:13].

Hallelujah! That really is "good news!" In case you're having trouble believing that the power of evil has been dealt with—listen to Jesus' reassuring words. . . .

> The time . . . has come . . . when Satan, the prince of this world, shall be cast out. And when I am lifted up I will draw everyone to me [John 12:31, 32].
>
> The evil prince of this world approaches. He has no power over me [John 14:30].
>
> There is deliverance from judgment because the prince of this world has already been judged [John 16:11].

Jesus has set his cross upon the head of Satan. Our Savior overcame the penalty and power of sin for us.

What a relief! Now we really can be good if we want to.

> For God took the sinless Christ and poured into him our

> sins. Then in exchange, he poured God's goodness into us [2 Cor. 5:21].

It's like a blood transfusion. Imagine yourself on a stretcher in the hospital. Next to you is the Son of God. A plastic tube runs from his arm to your arm. You watch his life-giving blood flow into your body. He literally sheds his blood so you can live the abundant life. Would you pull out the tube, jump off the stretcher, and run down the hall yelling, "No, Lord, I don't want your sacrifice! Leave me alone! I can live my life by myself! I don't need your help!"

Some people actually do this. They refuse the "new life" in Christ. They refuse his forgiveness! And they refuse his white robe of righteousness! They *choose* separation from God. They actually *choose* to go to hell.

> Don't you realize that you can choose your own master? You can choose sin (with death) or else obedience (with acquittal). The one to whom you offer yourself—he will take you and be your master and you will be his slave [Rom. 6:16].

> When the Holy Spirit controls our lives he will produce this kind of fruit in us: love, joy, peace, patience, kindness, goodness, faithfulness, gentleness and self-control [Gal. 5:22, 23].

FORMING A NEW PARTNERSHIP

If the "rules of the universe" demand that we love God, others, and ourselves—and if the "prince of this world" is out to pressure us into making wrong choices and bad judgments, then how do we strike up a partnership with the Holy Spirit so we can win this struggle between good and evil?

As I said in the Preface—when I first came to the Lord as a teenager, I had no idea of my rich inheritance in Christ. I did not know that those nine delicious fruits of the Spirit belonged to me. I did not know that my Lord's Holy Spirit came to dwell within me when I gave my life to Christ. All that time I had been unaware of the supernatural power within me. . . the power to be loving, the power to be joyful, the power to be peaceful, the power to be patient, the power to be good!

The Holy Spirit had always wanted to express these qualities through me, but I was trying to do it on my own.

...I tried to *love others*, but I couldn't even love myself. I always ran out of love. When the edges rubbed thin, I found it hard to forgive myself as well as others.

...I tried to project myself as a *joyful person*. I could keep my smile and laughter going for a little while, but then I'd run out of steam and fall into a depression.

...I tried to *act peaceful*, but as soon as my "worrywart" personality took off on its own, I became like a shaking leaf.

...I tried to *be patient* with my family, but when life didn't run smoothly, I lost my composure.

...I tried to *express kindness*, but when I was rebuffed, it hurt, and so I set up a wall of silence.

...I tried so hard to *be good* (to live by the letter of the law), but in the process I lost the spirit of the law.

Had I been acquainted with the Holy Spirit this would never have happened. Oh, how I must have grieved him all those years. But praise God—a precious little old lady, Corrie ten Boom, introduced me to the third person of the Trinity one night at a "Faith at Work" conference in Phoenix, Arizona. With her visual aids she showed me how I must be an "instrument" in the Lord's hands.

He the Battery—I the flashlight
He the Hand—I the glove
He the Ink—I the pen
He the Artist—I the canvas
He the Weaver—I the loom

Although my tapestry might look all "knotty" on the underneath side, my Father sees the upper side—the finished masterpiece. "Someday, he will show it to us," Corrie said. As I write today, Corrie is on the very threshhold of seeing her completed tapestry. With each new stroke she suffers, her soul draws closer and closer to her heavenly home where God will welcome her at the gates with open arms saying:

Corrie—your mansion is ready!
Corrie—how do you like your new body?
Corrie—I have a crown for your head!
Corrie—well done, my good and faithful servant.

How much I owe this precious Dutch woman who was obedient to God after her release from a German concentration camp—to "Go forth into all the world and tell others about the Father, Son, and Holy Spirit."

SPIRIT-FILLED LIVING

Now that I've met God's Holy Spirit, I am discovering how he wants to anoint my life in every area. Each day I pray that my husband and I will be surrendered and empowered by the fruit of God's Holy Spirit. I also know that God gives each one of us unique gifts to fit our personalities—for the purpose of:

1. Glorifying him.
2. Edifying the Body of Christ.
3. Uplifting our spiritual life.

We are beginning to recognize these gifts in one another and we are encouraging one another to use these gifts to the glory of God.

Recently I came across a *Guideposts* condensation of a book entitled, *If I Were Starting My Family Again*, by John M. Drescher (teacher, counselor, and father of five children).

I want to share with you an excerpt from John Drescher's book—followed by a true story that vividly illustrates his point.

> I remember a little fellow, frightened by the lightning and thunder, who called out one dark night, "Daddy, come. I'm scared!" "Oh, son," the father said, "God loves you and he'll take care of you." "I know God loves me and that he'll take care of me," the small son replied. "But right now, I want somebody who has skin on." [*Guideposts*, March 1979]

Once upon a time there was a mother and daddy who were "God's love with skin on" to their twelve-year-old son and fourteen-year-old daughter. Their final night together was spent on a very special "family outing." It was their daughter's birthday, so they went into town to see a popular stage play. They had a wonderful, memorable evening together.

Just two blocks from their home, a young, drunken driver ran a stop light and hit them broadside. The father was killed instantly—the mother died shortly thereafter. The son broke his arm and leg. The birthday girl escaped with only a couple of broken fingers. They were a dedicated Christian family, active in their church. At the memorial service they read from notes in the mother's Bible where she said, "The greatest thing in my life is my family and children." They were very loving and devoted parents.

When the little boy was told the news about his parents' death in his hospital bed, he looked up at his sister and said, "Some birthday." But she answered, "It was the most beautiful birthday I ever had. I shall never forget it." She was remembering the evening *before* the accident:

...the shared laughter
...the close togetherness
...the sense of belonging
...the unity they all felt in Christ.

In fourteen short years their parents had left an indelible legacy of love, joy, peace, patience, kindness, and goodness upon their children's lives.

Let each one of us determine to be "God's love with skin on"—to our families, our friends, and our relatives. Let God:

...smile through us
...hug through us
...kiss through us
...hold hands through us
...pray through us
...help through us
...love through us

Ask Jesus to fill you with the fruit of his Holy Spirit so you can practice *his goodness* and let it overflow onto others.

SEVEN
Taste the Fruit of FAITHFULNESS

Great is Thy faithfulness, O God my Father,
There is no shadow of turning with Thee.
Thou changest not, Thy compassions they fail not,
As Thou hast been Thou forever wilt be.

Summer and winter, and springtime and harvest,
Sun, moon, and stars in their courses above,
Join with all nature in manifold witness
To Thy great faithfulness, mercy and love.

Pardon for sin and a peace that endureth,
Thine own dear presence to cheer and to guide.
Strength for today and bright hope for tomorrow
Blessings all mine, with ten thousand besides!

Great is Thy faithfulness! Great is Thy faithfulness!
Morning by morning new mercies I see;
All I have needed Thy hand hath provided
Great is Thy faithfulness, Lord, unto me!

Thomas Chisholm, a Methodist life insurance agent, penned these words in the 1920s and William Runyon set the hymn to music. It became popular at Moody Bible Institute's chapel services, and later Billy Graham introduced it at his London Crusades. It also happens to be my husband's favorite hymn. Since he, like Chisholm, was once in the insurance business, perhaps they can better appreciate the "eternal promises" of this hymn. As E. Stanley Jones so often said, "We belong to an unchanging Christ and his unshakable kingdom."

The words of "Great Is Thy Faithfulness" are based on two passages of Scripture:

> Great is his faithfulness; his lovingkindness begins afresh each day [Lam. 3:23].
>
> Whatever is good and perfect comes to us from God, . . . and he shines forever without change or shadow [Jas. 1:17].

God's faithfulness is like that. He never grows tired or weary. He never falls asleep on the job! He is always watching over us.

> How precious it is, Lord, to realize that you are thinking about me constantly! I can't even count how many times a day your thoughts turn towards me. And when I waken in the morning, you are still thinking of me! [Psa. 139:17, 18].

Isn't it wonderful to realize that the Almighty Creator of the universe is that interested in us as individuals? There are billions of people here on Planet Earth—and yet he knows each one of us by *name.*

> Don't be afraid, for I have called you by *name*, you are mine! [Isa. 43:1].
>
> From within the womb he called me by *name* . . . [Isa. 49:1].
>
> I will not forget you. See, I have tattooed your *name* upon my palm [Isa. 49:16].

Not only does he know us by name, but he also knows:

. . . when we sit
. . . when we stand
. . . what we think
. . . when we need to stop and rest
. . . where we are
. . . what we're going to say
. . . he both precedes and follows us
. . . every day is recorded in his Book [Portions of Psalm 139].

This means that God has been "paying attention" to you and me for a long time—even before we knew and accepted him as our Lord and Savior. As I've said before, I was not aware of this until I was twenty-six—even though I had given Jesus my life at age thirteen. I am convinced there are a lot of people who don't know this. That is one of the two main reasons for writing this book:

1. A lot of *believers* have never been *taught* that it is possible to have a *daily relationship* with the Father through Jesus, and . . .
2. A lot of *nonbelievers* don't realize *God loves them* even though they ignore him.

Since I fell into the first category for many years, I was totally unaware of the "faithfulness" of God in my daily life.

Because I thought we had to struggle through this life on our own—doing the best we could—I ended up a bundle of frustrations, completely disillusioned and discouraged. I had no idea that from the very beginning, God had a special plan for my life. What an eye-opener when this concept began to unfold in my mind.

My first inkling that God was personally concerned with me was when he answered my prayer for a kindly doctor in the sanitarium. Early the next morning he sent a gray-haired, compassionate psychiatrist who gave me hope when he said, "*Believe* me, you *will* get well."

My second suspicion that God really cared was when I began to experience his unconditional love through the hospital staff. I really saw them as "angels." (Somehow God's helpers had gotten into that hospital.)

My third affirmation came through my husband's maturity in accepting me at my worst. Before this we often had bitter arguments over our tight budget. I refused to get a sitter so we could go out together, saying "We can't afford it." Now the doctors were saying, "You can't afford *not* to. So take a weekend pass, stay in a motel, court each other, rediscover one another."

God knew we needed this, too. He knew that when a couple have a baby on their nine-month anniversary and another baby on their second anniversary, there's not much time left for "getting to know one another." So in his faithfulness, God provided us with a "second chance"—a time to "honeymoon." When we began to realize that God really cared about our relationship as husband and wife, we no longer felt guilty about fitting "date nights" into our budget.

We were also learning that God's plan included a happy, fun-loving family. With a "new" daddy and mommy, this came almost naturally. As I said in the earlier chapters, we started to "play together" (sing songs, play games, go on fishing trips, attend church camps, take vacations). We also began to pray about little things as well as big things. We prayed about such things as:

...motel vacancies
...a wayside park for eating
...a restroom in the middle of the desert
...a runaway dog and cat
...a lost car key
...an economical restaurant
...firewood for our campsite

And as God began to answer some of our insignificant, specific prayers, we were overwhelmed. Like little children we had to "pinch" ourselves. God really *was* excited about everything we did. He went with us wherever we went. Psalm 139 was absolutely true! He did indeed "precede and follow us and place his hand of blessing on our heads."

We have hundreds of friends who have made this same discovery. What a joy it is to compare notes with them over the phone; at our talk-it-over groups; and on our vacations together with our brothers and sisters in the Lord. We've prayed our way up the coast, across the Hawaiian Islands, and throughout Israel. Between us we could fill a library with all the "serendipities" God has bestowed upon us.

> I will answer them before they even call to me. While they are still talking to me about their needs, I will go ahead and answer their prayers [Isa. 65:24].

One of the most joyful discoveries of our Christian walk has been the "closeness" of our Lord Jesus. After spending so many years worshiping a "far-off" God, it is like passing:

...from darkness into light;
...from make-believe into reality;
...from ancient history into current events;
...from death into life.

This "Family of God" is not just for heaven. Membership

is available right now! A Japanese pastor friend from Hawaii calls it "Kingdom living" and it has everything to do with the *faithfulness of God.* It means he wants to be involved in everything his children think, feel, say, and do.

BACKED BY HIS NAME

> Your promises are backed by all the honor of your name. When I pray, you answer me and encourage me by giving me the strength I need [Psa. 138:2, 3].

Perhaps you are saying, "Well, that's not the way it's been in my life! I can't see any evidence that God is interested in what happens to me." But let me assure you that he *is* (even if you're not aware of it), and someday he will show you how all the pieces fit together. Then you will exclaim with the hymn writer, "Great is Thy faithfulness, Lord unto me."

Let me share with you how God's faithfulness surrounds us from the moment of our birth, even when we don't know about it.

GOD'S FAITHFULNESS INSTRUCTS US

God Uses Parents

> Listen to your father and mother. What you learn from them will stand you in good stead; it will gain you many honors [Prov. 1:9].

I was blessed with good, churchgoing parents, who felt it was important to take their children to God's house every week. Although we were too shy to share our faith with one another, we believed in God and tried to live according to Christian ethics. From my father and mother I learned:

Conscientiousness: I saw my daddy spend many hours on his job. He always wanted to "do his best." He could be depended on to "give it all he had."

Concern: I saw my mother show deep concern for our invalid grandmother who spent many years living in our home. I watched her feed her, bathe her, entertain her.

Commitment: I saw my daddy give a lot of his free time to the church, helping in the financial department and administering communion to the congregation.

Hard Work: I saw both my parents work very hard around the house—cleaning, landscaping, weeding, canning, painting, etc.

Honesty: I saw my daddy's honesty in his dealings with people. He was a very transparent, vulnerable man.

Helpfulness: I saw my mother's helpfulness in doing favors for people in need (cleaning their houses, cooking a meal, nursing them back to health).

Creativity: I saw both my parents work creatively on home and church projects (programs, crafts, dramas, talks).

These are the strengths I picked up as a little girl—burying them deep within my subconscious. In addition to serving as an example of Christianity in action, my parents also made it possible for me to take piano, trumpet, singing, dancing, and elocution lessons. The discipline of study helped me in teaching and writing later on.

Maybe your parents were not Christians; maybe they argued and fought most of the time; maybe they even separated or died when you were very young. Does this mean you are warped for life—doomed to suffer the consequences of your environment? Not when you depend on the faithfulness of God.

...He can redeem parent's mistakes (and we all make them).
...He can bridge the gap of love (if you didn't get enough).
...He can fill you with compasson (if you experienced loneliness yourself).
...He can give you the desire to create a happy home (if yours was not).
...He can enable you to become the kind of a parent you always wished you had had.
...He can inspire you to look to him (even though you never did before).

So even the bad and sad times of life can be "used" by God to turn you into the kind of a person he wants you to become.

...sorrow can make you more compassionate.
...pain can make you more tender.
...loneliness can make you more aware of people who are hurting.
...anger can spur you on to constructive and creative corrections.

...fear and guilt can drive you into the arms of Grace.

> Because of our faith he has brought us into this place of highest privilege where we now stand, and we confidently and joyfully look forward to actually becoming all that God had in mind for us to be [Rom. 5:2].

God Uses the Scriptures

Not only does God use all kinds of parents to "instruct" us but he also uses the Bible.

> The whole Bible was given to us by inspiration from God and is useful to teach us what is true and to make us realize what is wrong in our lives; it straightens us out and helps us do what is right. It is God's way of making us well prepared at every point, fully equipped to do good to everyone [2 Tim. 3:16, 17].

I received my first Bible from my parents. It was the red-lettered King James Version, and it had my name on it. I still have it. It's underlined and stuffed with precious momentoes. I will pass it on to my children someday.

But when I was in the sanitarium, I could no longer read my Bible, so I depended on Norman Vincent Peale's "thought conditioners" for my spiritual food. As those positive Scripture verses sank into my subconscious mind, they began to work on my raw emotions. Fear, anger, guilt, and grief started to dissolve in the healing forgiveness of God's Word. As I got better and returned to the church, Ken Taylor's *Living Letters* was released—followed by the Gospels, Prophets, and Books of Moses. One by one we bought each new edition, until we finally were able to get the entire Living Bible. It read like a modern-day story—the message was so clear! I understood passages I had never understood before. I began giving these Bibles away to family and friends—even ministers and doctors. Ken Taylor, who originally paraphrased the Bible for his ten children, has taken a lot of criticism, but I am convinced there will be many in heaven because they met Jesus in the pages of *The Living Bible*, and as a result committed their lives to him as their Lord and Savior.

It's never too late to read your Bible from cover to cover.

Whatever Bible translation you have, if it has introduced you to its Author (God, your Father; Jesus, your Lord and Savior; and the Holy Spirit, your Guide and Counselor), then cherish it as your own special "love letter" from heaven. Read it, study it, meditate upon it, and share it!

God Uses Preachers and Teachers

> If you are a teacher, do a good job of teaching. If you are a preacher, see to it that your sermons are strong and helpful [Rom. 12:7, 8].

The world is full of preachers and teachers. Some live up to this Scripture admonition—others do not. We are warned to use discernment in whom we listen to. There will always be false prophets upon the scene, but the Lord says we "shall know them by their fruits." Check what they say in accordance with Scripture and beware of pharisaical hypocrites. Jesus had them in his day—we have them in ours. But God's faithfulness is continually weeding out the deceivers. Listen to some of God's penetrating statements in Jeremiah and Ezekiel, which apply just as much today as they did then.

> Don't listen to these false prophets when they prophesy to you, filling you with futile hopes. They are making up everything they say. They do not speak for me! They keep saying to these rebels who despise me, "Don't worry! All is well!" and to those who live the way they want to, "The Lord has said you shall have peace!" But can you name even one of these prophets who lives close enough to God to hear what he is saying? Has even one of them cared enough to listen? . . . I have not sent these prophets, yet they claim to speak for me; I gave them no message, yet they say their words are mine. If they were mine, they would try to turn my people from their evil ways. . . . So I stand against these "prophets" who get their messages from each other—these smooth-tongued prophets who say, "This message is from God!" Their made-up dreams are flippant lies that lead my people into sin. I did not send them and they have no message at all for my people, says the Lord [Portions of Jeremiah 23].
>
> Woe to the shepherds who feed themselves instead of

> their flocks. Shouldn't shepherds feed the sheep? You eat the best food and wear the finest clothes, but you let your flocks starve. You haven't taken care of the weak nor tended the sick nor bound up the broken bones nor gone looking for those who have wandered away and are lost. I will hold them responsible for what has happened to my flock. I will take away their right to feed the flock [Portions of Ezekiel 34:2-10].

So be careful—test the message with Scripture. Is it "man's opinion" or is it "God's Truth"? The Holy Spirit is the real Teacher and when he anoints God's yielded servants, they will preach and teach with the authority of God. From them we will learn what God wants us to know. Being imperfect human instruments, a little "self will" still slips in, but when both teacher and student are aware of this, the Lord will help us sift out his nuggets of truth. Being a teacher myself, I am well aware of the statement in James that warns:

> Dear brothers [and sisters], don't be too eager to tell others their faults, for we all make mistakes; and when we teachers of religion, who should know better, do wrong, our punishment will be greater than it would be for others [Jas. 3:1].

This keeps me on my toes and willing to admit my mistakes, since I know we all have our "feet of clay."

GOD'S FAITHFULNESS CORRECTS US

God's Built-In Consequences

Let's look at the subject of eating. Do we eat to live or do we live to eat? America is full of overweight, overfed people—and many of them are Christians. Listen to Brother Paul's comments on overeating:

> I can do anything I want to if Christ has not said no, but some of these things aren't good for me. Even if I am allowed to do them, I'll refuse to if I think they might get such a grip on me that I can't easily stop when I want to. For instance, take the matter of eating. God has given us an appetite for food and stomachs to digest it. But that doesn't mean we should eat more than we need. Don't think of eating as important,

> because some day God will do away with both stomachs and food [1 Cor. 6:12, 13].

Ever since our third son was born I've been "innocently" adding one pound per year until recently he turned fifteen—and I found myself fifteen pounds overweight. I've made attempts at dieting and exercising, but have not been consistent. And so the scale has stayed about the same for a long time. I kept praying for God to help me lose weight through diet and exercise, but I failed to cooperate with him in the process. Obviously the pounds don't just drop off by themselves.

By eating too much of the wrong kinds of food and not exercising regularly, I began to feel stuffed and mentally sluggish. One night at a musical, following a big dinner in a restaurant, I almost fell asleep in my seat. As I fought sleep and watched the dancers flit across the stage, I began remembering my younger years as a dance major at the university. I thought, "I'm too young to feel this old!" That very week I marched myself into an exercise studio, weighed in, got measured all over, squeezed into a powder blue leotard and began my stretching and groaning—in conjunction with a twenty-four-hour fast and the elimination of sugar, salt, and carbohydrates. This time I was determined to stick with it—but it was "God's built-in consequences" (stuffiness and sluggishness) that intensified my desire to "eat right" and "exercise right." The end result—I now look better, feel better, and will undoubtedly live longer. Praise God for his faithful reminder!

God's Built-In Corrections

Several years ago I was having some unexplainable pains in my legs and back. My moods seemed to fluctuate irregularly. I felt sad most of the time. We were undergoing some deep-seated tensions among our family and friends (divorce, cancer, coma, loss of employment, estrangements, heavy teaching assignments, speaking commitments, long-term house guests, people needing counseling, etc.). I figured my symptoms were all psychosomatic, so tried just to grin and bear it. Our family doctor had said my hysterectomy might have some physiological side effects, so if I felt I needed it, he would give me a hormone shot that would last for five or six months. I took him up on his offer, and the very next day I felt worse—as I had when I was in the sanitarium twenty-five years before (full of anxiety, fears, and depression). Later I learned that "one in ten women will find her symptoms *increase* in severity when she takes hormones. . . ." *(For Women Only* by Petersen & Petersen).

I ran to my pastor in tears. What could I do about all those women who were expecting their teacher to return to class? "We'll just change the game plan," Dr. Schuller said. "You take a rest and we'll find a substitute. I'm convinced you are not as sick as you were the first time. Your 'memories' are just playing tricks on you. God has healed you, and he's allowing you to remember what it feels like to be depressed. You've helped a lot of women love their Bible and face their emotions. 'He who began a good work in you will complete it' (Phil. 1:6)."

I was relieved that my ladies had been taken care of, but my own "hellish" symptoms lasted for seven more weeks. During that time I "preached" to myself, listened to tapes, read my Bible, devotional books, and psychology books; forced myself to sing at the piano; took long walks; swam laps in the pool; tried to eat fruit and drink Jell-o; and talked out loud to God day and night—shouting Scriptures to the enemy every time a negative thought or word entered my mind. I kept a journal of my daily feelings and insights. Friends wrote and came to encourage me.

But self-treatment is not the *only* answer for depression (especially when it continues for over thirty days); and so I finally sought the aid of a Christian psychiatrist. I felt like I was admitting defeat, especially when he prescribed an anti-depressant. At first I would not swallow the medication at home—I just put it under my tongue and spit it out when my husband wasn't looking. I thought it would somehow be sacreligious to use medicine as a "crutch" now that I was a Bible teacher. When I finally admitted this to my doctor, he gave me a physiological explanation of how the medication would correct a hormone imbalance in my spinal fluid. He assured me Jesus would not think less of me for using medication. But he also leveled with me that I was "highly prejudiced against emotional illness in myself." If this were true, then I had some "self-forgiving" to do. In the weeks that followed, the medication began to have a positive effect upon my mental attitude. I could legitimately smile again, laugh again, sing again, read again, and pray again. I was beginning to feel like my old self. Now my doctor and I could more clearly reflect upon my priorities and rearrange my life style where it needed rearranging.

...I learned that sometimes I needed to say "No" and other times I needed to say "Yes." Just a simple, "Yes, I will," or "No, I won't" (Matt. 5:37). I needed to respect my limitations and assess my abilities—seeking God's discernment in the process.

...I learned that sometimes I had been too passive—and needed to speak up with my feelings and convictions. ("Be angry but do not sin. Do not let the sun go down on your anger. . . .") It's healthy to get our anger out into the open where we can deal with it constructively—so we "do not give a mighty foothold to the devil" (Eph. 4:26) and turn it inward on ourselves.

...I learned that sometimes I needed to put my study books aside and take time to "play." "It is senseless for you to work so hard from early morning until late at night...for God wants his loved ones to get their proper rest" (Psa. 127:2).

...I learned that the well-balanced life (physical, mental, spiritual, and social) is scripturally sound!

...So Jesus grew both tall [physical]
...and wise [mental]
...and was loved by God [spiritual]
...and man [social] [Luke 2:52].

Through this illness God's faithfulness corrected more of my weak areas and impressed upon me the importance of living the well-rounded life.

GOD'S FAITHFULNESS INSPIRES US

Mountaintop Experiences

I praise God from the bottom of my heart and soul for every camp, conference, and retreat experience he has given me.

From the sand dunes of Michigan to the ocean shore of Honolulu to the desert trails of Judea, I have felt the impact of God's majesty, the tenderness of his Son and the indwelling power of his Holy Spirit.

When John, James, and Peter had their mountaintop experience with Jesus at the time of his transfiguration, they knew they'd never forget those glorious moments together. God gives us all moments like these so we will remember them when we get discouraged or lose hope! They keep us going and fill us with inspiration.

...I still see 500 young people atop a Michigan sand dune at sunset—all praying out loud at the same time. I see us winding down the pathway after dark by flashlight—like twinkling stars in the night.

...I still see seven families giving their testimony in a little Japanese church on the Kona Coast. I see us taking hands with the congregation and praying for miracles.

...I still see our tour group prayerfully pausing in the Garden of Gethsemane and at the Garden Tomb as we remembered what our Lord did for us there.

Human Saints

Whether we meet them in person, in a book, or in a movie, these "human saints" inspire us with their living testimony. Their closeness to Jesus is so evident that just being around them causes some of this "charisma" to rub off on us.

...Some of my camp and conference leaders were my teenage "heroes." I wanted to grow up and be like them.

...Some of my pastors and teachers inspired me to be more like Jesus.

...Some elderly ladies and gentlemen in my churches taught me about humility and surrender.

...Some Christian writers filled me with excitement and determination to let God use me.

...Some Christian speakers challenged me to let God live his life through me.

Don't let a single month pass by without reading a Christian book or listening to a Christian speaker or tape. And don't let a single year pass by without attending a "mountaintop adventure." Inspiration is one of the best "spiritual shots in the arm" a Christian can get.

GOD'S FAITHFULNESS PROTECTS US

> The Lord is my fort where I can enter and be safe; no one can follow me in and slay me. He is a rugged mountain where I hide; he is my Savior, a rock where none can reach me, and a tower of safety. He is my shield. He is like the strong horn of a mighty fighting bull. All I need to do is cry to him—oh, praise the Lord—and I am saved from my enemies! In my distress I screamed to the Lord for his help. And he heard me from heaven; my cry reached his ears. . . . He reached down from heaven and took me and drew me out of my great trials. He rescued me from deep waters. He delivered me from my strong enemy. . . . the Lord held me steady. He led me to a place of safety, for he delights in me. The Lord rewarded me for doing right and being pure. . . . What a God he is! How perfect in every way! All his promises prove true. He is a shield for everyone who hides behind him. For who is God except our Lord? Who but he is as a rock? He fills me with strength and protects me wherever I go. . . . You have given me your salvation as my shield. Your right hand, O Lord, supports me; your gentleness has made me great. You have made wide steps beneath my feet so that I need never slip. . . . God is alive! Praise him who is the great rock of protection [Portions of Psalm 18].

Can you place yourself in the Psalmist's sandals? Can you remember a time when God was your fort, your rugged mountain, your rock, your tower, your shield? Have you ever cried out in distress and felt God's hand take hold of yours? Have you felt his steadiness as he led you to a place of safety? Has he ever made "wide steps beneath your feet" so you wouldn't stumble? Is he your "great rock of protection?"

In the New Testament, Jesus also has some very precious words for God's children to take to heart. He assures us that "his sheep" are *protected* by the Father and himself:

> My sheep recognize my voice and I *know* them and

> they follow me. I give them eternal life and they shall never perish. No one shall snatch them away from me, for my Father has given them to me, and he is more powerful than anyone else, so no one can kidnap them from me. I and the Father are one [John 10:27-30].

Armor for Battle

Here on earth a battle is taking place between good and evil. God is the source of all goodness, and Satan is the source of all that is evil. You and I are often the "battleground," but we have someone to fight our battles for us. Brother Paul tells us about God's faithfulness in times like these:

> I want to remind you that your strength must come from the Lord's mighty power within you. Put on all of God's armor so that you will be able to stand safe against all strategies and tricks of Satan. For we are not fighting against people made of flesh and blood, but against persons without bodies—the evil rulers of the unseen world, those mighty satanic beings and great evil princes of darkness who rule this world: and against huge numbers of wicked spirits in the spirit world [Eph. 6:10-12].

So all we need to do is put on the whole armor of God in the proper order.

...The *belt* of truth (which tells us we belong to God because of Jesus' sacrifice).

...The *breastplate* of God's approval (which reminds us he has made us righteous).

...The *shoes* to preach Good News (which enables us to witness).

...The *shield* of faith (which provides for our defeat of Satan's tricks and accusations).

...The *helmet* of salvation (which assures us that no one can snatch us from the Father).

...The *sword* of the Spirit (which gives us the Word of God to quote to Satan) [Eph. 6:14-17].

When we wear this spiritual armor every day, no one can trip us up. Temptation can be nipped in the bud; negative feelings and thoughts can be dissipated; and our consciences can be kept clean and pure.

GOD'S WARNING

Only those who reject the Lord have reason to fear:

> For you closed your eyes to the facts and did not choose to reverence and trust the Lord, and you turned your back on me, spurning my advice. That is why you must eat the bitter fruit of having your own way, and experience the full terrors of the pathway you have chosen [Prov. 1:29-31].

When this happens over and over again, the heart hardens and after awhile there is no longer any "tenderness" towards God. God's faithfulness never gives up on man, but sometimes men "choose" to give up on God. This is the deepest tragedy of all! This is why evangelists will preach "repentance" till their dying day. Conversion (turning away from sin towards God) is truly a matter of eternal life or death because our righteous Father cannot tolerate sin. It has to be confessed and cleansed at the cross.

GOD'S ASSURANCE

But let me just say a word to anyone who has made his "confession of faith," and is still not *convinced* he has been accepted by God. I was in the same predicament until an evangelist friend (Joe Blinco) gave me this beautiful illustration.

> "Mary Lee, when you married your husband, you were *really* married! Maybe you didn't '*feel*' like it right away, but that didn't alter the fact. You didn't have to run back to the church and get remarried over and over again. You might want to renew your vows as a sign of your recommitment, but you were legally married the first time you said, 'I Do.' . . . This is how it is with your decision to follow Christ. When you gave yourself to God, He took you just as you were. You don't have to keep returning to the altar for another conversion experience. You are His and He is yours! You can re-dedicate yourself to the Lord on a daily basis, but you belong to Him for all eternity."

Now we can look forward to the salvation God has promised us. There is no longer any room for doubt,

> and we can tell others that salvation is ours, for there is no question that he will do what he says [Heb. 10:23].

PASS IT ON

So you see, God's faithfulness is there all the time—in the beginning, in the end, and forever after. God's faithfulness instructs us, corrects us, inspires us, and protects us. All we need to do is receive it and respond in faithfulness to others.

> Are you a wise and *faithful* servant of the Lord? Have I given you the task of managing my household, to feed my children day by day? Blessings on you if I return and find you *faithfully* doing your work. I will put such *faithful* ones in charge of everything I own! [Matt. 24:45-47].

Ask Jesus to fill you with the fruit of his Holy Spirit so you can truly understand his divine faithfulness.

EIGHT
Taste the Fruit of GENTLENESS

Lord, thou knowest better than I know myself that I am growing older and will someday be old. Keep me from the fatal habit of thinking I must say something on every subject and on every occasion. Release me from craving to straighten out everybody's affairs. Make me thoughtful but not moody, helpful but not bossy. With my vast store of wisdom, it seems a pity not to use it all, but thou knowest, Lord, that I want a few friends at the end.

Keep my mind free from the recital of endless details; give me wings to get to the point. Seal my lips on my aches and pains. They are increasing and the love of rehearsing them is becoming sweeter as the years go by. I dare not ask for grace enough to enjoy the tales of others' pains but help me to endure them with patience.

I dare not ask for improved memory but for a growing humility and a lessening cocksureness when my memory seems to clash with the memories of others. Teach me the glorious lesson that occasionally I may be mistaken.

Keep me reasonably sweet; I do not want to be a saint—some of them are so hard to live with—but a sour old person is one of the crowning works of the devil. Give me the ability to see good things in unexpected places and talents in unexpected people. And give me, Lord, the grace to tell them so.

Amen

Do you want to be that kind of a person when you grow older? Do you know any "grandmas" and "grandpas" that fit that category now? Maybe you already qualify for that distinctive honor yourself. Being a "gentle-man" or a "gentle-woman" takes lots and lots of practice. If we don't start when we're young and middle-aged, we'll never turn out like the author of this prayer. Instead of being gentle and fun to be around in our senior years, we'll likely become:

...overly talkative
...preachy
...moody
...bossy
...overbearing
...bragging
...even obnoxious.

If, on the other hand, we want people to welcome our presence, then we must nourish a gentle spirit—one that will bring joy and peace everywhere we go! Brother Peter has some beautiful words from God on this subject. He says:

> Be beautiful inside, in your hearts, with the lasting charm of a *gentle* and *quiet spirit* which is so precious to God [1 Pet. 3:4].

I like that, don't you? Does that describe you? This year I've been praying for the fruit of "gentleness" to manifest itself in the life of our family. I've been watching for results, and already I can see God's hand at work—taming us one by one. These are some of my discoveries (based on a portion of Colleen Townsend's book, *A New Joy,* Fleming H. Revell, 1973).

Gentle people don't fight and argue with God because they know his ways are the best ways. They've learned to trust him.

...Our little girl was eliminated in the high school cheer-leading finals, but she wrote a friend, "God must have something else he wants me to do."

...Our number three son got laid off from his part-time job when the "older boys" came home for the summer, but he responded, "That's OK. I'll find another job that's even better."

Gentle people are both "tough and tender" with a gentle strength and power.

...Our number one son really puts his water polo boys through their paces bright and early every morning, but he has time after school hours to sit and talk with his team at their "Aqua-Spirit" sessions.

...Our number two son flies supersonic jets for the USAF, but at the end of a day he cuddles his little ones on his lap and gives them the TLC they desire.

Gentle people are adaptable. They move with the rhythm of life, roll with the punches, accept interruptions. They aren't rigid!

...My husband is like this. He is always a willing chauffeur and tour guide for senior citizens, foreign visitors, or out-of-town company. People are more important than schedules to him. He has a knack for making them feel like he has nothing more important to do than entertain them. (As I write this, he just finished doing this for four grandmas and grandpas and a family of tourists over Father's Day.)

...I've become more and more adaptable the longer I live with my husband. The things I feared to do he talks me into "trying." He has shown me that interruptions are God's way of breaking my workaholic cycle. He has taught me the importance of taking "mini-vacations."

Gentle people are yielded to God. They give him their best and he gives them his best. They become instruments in his hands.

...I've seen this happen over and over again in our lives as we allow him to use our inborn talents for his glory (writing, speaking, organizing meetings and conferences, taking tests, planning parties, vacations, and entertaining house guests).

Gentle people allow God to soften them—their tongues, tempers, egos, etc.

...I've seen brother and sister nip an argument in the bud by refusing to snap back—by adding a bit of gentle humor. (Not always, but sometimes.)

...I've seen members of the family walk away from a tense situation until they cool down, so they can return to the situation with wisdom and common sense. (Not 100 percent yet, but it's improving.)

Gentle people don't scold, nag or pout.

...I'm watching myself change from a "nagger" into an "inspirer" when it comes to my children's rooms, their choice of music, my husband's diet, and his aversion to yard work.

Gentle people are emotionally controlled. They don't fly off the handle and make a fool of themselves.

...I've observed our younger two mature in the handling of their disappointments and frustrations at school and with their friends.

Gentle people are teachable. They ask questions and learn something new every day.

...I've been aware of God's daily schoolroom. Instead of questioning "Why?" or "How come?" he's teaching us to ask, "What are you trying to tell us?" Or, "What do you want us to learn?" He always come through with new insights as we grow in the midst of life's experiences.

Gentle people have a sensitive spirit towards other people's hurts and disappointments, rather than wearing their own hearts on their sleeves.

...I've rejoiced every time I've seen a member of our family hurt when another hurts, cry when another cries, ache when another aches. Walking in each other's shoes at home prepares us to do this everywhere we go.

Gentle people are creative. As our pastor says, they know how to turn:

"Problems into projects;
obstacles into opportunities;
stumbling blocks into stepping stones."

And so,

...a "blah" bathroom gets panelled in scrap lumber by our fifteen-year-old son.

...our fourteen-year-old daughter raises low grades to high

grades in order to earn a private telephone.

...a defeat makes our son's water polo team work harder to win the next game.

...insights our family has gained through illness help us inspire others.

Gentleness is not only *taught*, it is also *caught* by watching "gentle people" in action.

Recently I was standing in line at a health cafeteria, listening to the couple ahead of me hassle and criticize the girl behind the counter who was taking their order. Each time she retorted with a gentle and quiet spirit, but they never melted. Even at the table they continued to find fault with everything. At the close of the meal they got up and left their empty paper plates on the table (even though this was a self-service cafe). But when I noticed the sour expressions on their faces as compared to the cheerful expression on the girl behind the counter, I realized why Jesus had said:

> Happy are those who are meek [gentle] for they shall inherit the earth.

It was true. She was in harmony with God's game plan—the crabby couple was not!

Last week my heart sank after a phone call from a sister in Christ. She told me that the husband of one of our Bible study students had just been stabbed to death over the noon hour at his place of business. (Motive: robbery!) How could anybody be so heartless—so cruel? Our friend's husband was a warm and gentle grandfather who loved his Lord and family very much. Was this a reversal of Christ's third Beatitude? Our friend was meek and now he was dead. His killer was evil and wasn't caught. "It's not fair," we cry. "Aren't the gentle suppose to inherit the earth?"

God answers, Wait and see! My own Son was murdered by evil men, too, but I turned his bad Friday into a Good Friday—for the salvation of many. His sacrifice brought you into the Family of God.

Could anything positive come out of anything as evil as a murder? Yes, if you and I vow to do something about the evil forces in this world that are hardening the hearts of thousands—robbing them of all gentleness.

Let's look at a few of these forces:

...violence on TV is gradually destroying any natural inclination towards tenderness and compassion in our young children.

...murders and rapes in the movies are gradually destroying all respect for the sanctity of life and love in our young people.

...pornography is playing on warped minds and often excites vicious behavior.

...pushers, prostitutes, and pimps selling drugs and sex are destroying the minds and bodies of every age.

The person who murdered my friend's husband grew up in this kind of world. Day by day, week by week, month by month, and year by year his heart was hardened and gentleness crushed. It's like putting live frogs in lukewarm water. By turning the heat up gradually, they don't even realize they're being cooked. Before they know it—it's too late to jump out (they're too far gone). This is what is happening to our world. Many people are being "boiled alive" and they don't even know it. Even in some of our "good homes," men, women, boys, and girls are becoming less compassionate than they were a couple decades ago.

The other night Erma Bombeck spoke up against violence in her column—"Open Letter to Everyone Who Has Produced or Defended Violence on TV."

> You don't remember me, do you? I'm the viewer who used to sit in front of a television set and when a gun was fired, I nearly jumped out of my chair. When I saw someone begin beaten, instinctively I flinched and felt the pain. Or when I saw blood, I turned my head away and my stomach felt funny.
>
> I know I don't seem like the same person you remembered.
>
> I'm not.
>
> You have desensitized me. During a single evening, I once saw twelve people shot to death, two people tortured (one a child), one dumped in a swimming pool, two cars explode with people in them, a rape and a man who crawled three blocks with a knife in his stomach.
>
> And you know something? I didn't feel shock or horror. I didn't feel excitement or repugnance. I didn't

> feel pity or sadness. I didn't even feel anger.
>
> The truth is, I didn't feel. And I hate you for it. Through repeated assault of one violent act after another you have taken from me something which I valued . . . something that contributed to my compassion and caring . . . the instinct to feel.

But before it ever gets to this stage, let's do all in our power to counteract the violence, cruelty, and ugliness we encounter every day with tenderness, compassion,and beauty.

BRING GENTLENESS INTO OUR WORLD BY COUNTERACTING VIOLENCE WITH TENDERNESS.

1. One of the best ways to teach a child *tenderness* is through the care of a pet—bird, kitten, puppy, horse, hamster, duck, or bunny to name a few. Having an animal they can pet and talk to, feed, and care for—teaches them "unselfishness." Of course you have to get involved in the process with them in order for them to learn how. You encourge them in their care, but you do *not* "take over" for them. (I've done the latter and then the child misses all the benefits.)

2. Baby brothers and sisters help instill *tenderness* if you incorporate the older children's assistance in the proper way. "Taking care of baby" can be a chore or it can be a lot of fun. Our eleven- and twelve-year-olds used to love to "show off" their little brother and sister to friends and school chums; but when they reached the dating age, they preferred we "hire" a sitter.

3. Visiting nursing homes and hospitals can encourage *tenderness* as you reach out to "cheer up" lonely patients. Our little girl cried the first time we took her on one of our weekly visits. She felt "so sorry for the sick people." When a nurse assured her that her songs and smile gave them something to look forward to—she was happy to return.

4. Baby sitting can help our young people grow in *tenderness* if they're taught how to perform the role maturely. Many are better mothers and fathers themselves for having learned how to care for other people's children.

5. Handicapped children often bring forth *tenderness* in

other members of the family. I've seen a little five-year-old clean her crippled brother's glasses, push his wheelchair, and fetch his toys. I've seen another five-year-old listen patiently while her deaf sister tried to make herself understood. I've seen teenagers decide to go into one of the "helping" professions because a member of their family was handicapped. I've seen stoic, systematic daddies bow their heads in prayer over sick children. I've seen mothers spend all day patterning and exercising their crippled little ones.

When we and our children are exposed to some of these suggestions, we will be counteracting all the violence of the world with a little bit of tenderness. When we feed our computers with "TLC memories" we will turn into gentle people.

> Is there any such thing as Christians cheering each other up? . . . Are your hearts tender and sympathetic at all? Then make me truly happy by loving each other and agreeing wholeheartedly with each other, working together with one heart and mind and purpose. . . . Don't just think about your own affairs, but be interested in others, too, and in what they are doing. [Portions of Philippians 2:1-4].

BRING GENTLENESS INTO OUR WORLD BY COUNTERACTING CRUELTY WITH COMPASSION.

Compassion—like tenderness—is grown and developed. It doesn't just happen by accident. We are all born with a natural tendency to "want what we want when we want it."

...as babies we hollered when we wanted someone to do something for us.

...as toddlers we yelled when a visiting toddler took our favorite toy.

...as grade schoolers we pouted when we lost a ball game.

...as high schoolers we cried when our friends let us down.

...as adults we often get depressed if life doesn't go our way.

"Poor me!" we respond. Now that doesn't mean we necessarily become cruel just because we can't always have our own way; but it does mean we spend a lot more time thinking about ourselves than we do thinking about others. In extreme cases, a life centered on oneself *could* result in cruelty:

...wanting money, they rob and kill
...wanting sex, they rape
...wanting success, they walk all over their competitors
...wanting power, they sell their souls
...wanting prestige, they compromise their principles
...wanting possessions, they distort their priorities.

Many psychologists and theologians say that the root cause of self-absorption is a deep lack of self-worth. In trying to "prove" they are somebody important, they get into all kinds of trouble. What it all boils down to is they lack compassion for themselves as well as for others. Unable to love themselves, they are unable to love their fellow men. Without compassion, there can be no gentleness! The two go hand in hand! Jesus was the most compassionate person who ever lived, and he came to earth to show us our Father's compassion in action.

> We need have no fear of someone who loves us perfectly; his perfect love for us eliminates all dread of what he might do to us. If we are afraid, it is for fear of what he might do to us, and shows that we are not fully convinced that he really loves us [1 John 4:18].

> He was wounded and bruised for our sins. He was chastised that we might have peace; he was lashed—and we were healed! . . . Because of what he experienced, my righteous Servant shall make many to be counted righteous before God, for he shall bear all their sins [Portions of Isaiah 53].

> Only those who have the Holy Spirit within them can understand what the Holy Spirit means. Others just can't take it in. But the spiritual man has insight into everything, and that bothers and baffles the man of the world who can't understand him at all. How could he? For certainly he has never been one to know the Lord's thoughts, or to discuss them with him, or to move the hands of God by prayer. But strange as it seems, we Christians actually do have within us a portion of the very thoughts and mind of Christ [1 Cor. 2:14b-16].

We can begin to counteract cruelty with compassion the same way God does—first in the home, then in the community, then in the world. When this happens, a "gentle spirit" will move across the face of this earth.

Compassion at Home

Tensions and frustrations at home demand an outlet! If we never talk about what "bugs" us or hurts us, the problems will eventually flare up in temper explosions and angry words. If we want a gentle atmosphere at home we must work at it. Several avenues have opened themselves to our family.

Family Talk Time: We play a game called the "Ungame." We take turns selecting a card with a subjective question on it.

...What is the biggest mistake you ever made in your life?
...What is something that makes you feel sad?
...If you were told you only had one week to live, how would you spend it?
...What do you like most about yourself? Least?
...What one thing besides love do you want to give your children?
...In one line, what is life all about?

As you can see, the questions are specific as well as general. They are designed to make you think and get at your feelings. All ages can play the game and you can add questions of your own.

Family Devotions: In nearly thirty years of family life, we have had a variety of devotional formats in order to maintain enthusiasm.

...Children's Bible stories with question and answer time.
...Selecting Scripture verses from a "Promise Box."
...Reading a specific book in the Bible (such as one of the Gospels, Psalms, Proverbs, James, and 1 John).
...Keeping a Scripture "recipe" box and placing the cards we are memorizing in a conspicuous place (refrigerator, mirror, door, etc.).
...Reading from devotional books and inspirational magazines.

...Listening to Bible study tapes and answering questions in our notebooks.
...Hand holding, hugging, or huddle prayers when we say goodbye in the morning or send someone off on a trip.
...Kneeling by the bedside or at our living room worship center.
...Open-eye praying in restaurants or as we travel by car on vacation times.
...Seaside sanctuary worship services.
...Fireside sing-alongs.
...Moonlight "thank you" prayers in tents and trailers.
...Telephone prayers.
...Letter prayers.

Let your imagination create unique variations to suit your particular family needs. What works when the children are little may not be practical when the children are older and busier. Ask God to inspire you with ideas. Remember, compassionate communication can produce a "gentle spirit" in our homes.

Compassion in the Community

With misunderstandings occurring at the office, in the schools, and in the neighborhoods where we live, God has shown us a solution for "compassionate communication" outside the immediate family circle.

Small Groups. About sixteen years ago God introduced us to "sharing groups." We meet every two weeks for the purpose of:
...learning to let Jesus love us
...learning to love others unconditionally
...learning to listen deeply
...learning to leave our mistakes at the cross
...learning to lean on the Holy Spirit
...learning to lead others to the Lord.

These informal "laboratories in living" are teaching us how to become more compassionate communicators with one another so we can more easily apply these principles in the outside communities where we live.

Compassion in the World

Our world has become a "neighborhood" with the speed of jets and the projectile reality of nuclear weapons. We either learn to live together or we blow up together. God has shown us some solutions that begin with us.

Live-In Houseguests. For twenty years now we have been inviting the "world" into our home so that we could relate to people of other cultures and backgrounds. Men and women from Korea, Japan, and Burma have lived with us for several months—teaching us more than we could ever learn in books. (This summer a sixteen-year-old German girl will make her home with us for eight weeks.)

Cultural-Exchange Programs. These programs have enabled our family to fellowship with people from all over Asia, Europe, Africa, and South America as they join us for meals, picnics, and outings. Friendships with foreign visitors have enabled us to put our arms around the world.

BRING GENTLENESS INTO OUR WORLD BY COUNTERACTING UGLINESS WITH BEAUTY.

God created a beautiful world for us to live in. He thought of everything:

...air to breathe
...water to drink
...food to eat
...sunshine to warm us
...breezes to cool us
...moonlight to make us romantic.

The list is endless! God's handiwork is all around us! But sometimes it gets squeezed out by the handiwork of men. True, man is made in the image of God with the ability also to create "works of beauty"; but, sad to say, he sometimes produces "works of ugliness:"

...a littered beach
...a contaminated stream
...a yardful of weeds
...a run-down house
...garbage in the streets and alleys

...butchered forests
...tar-soaked fowls.

Once again the list is endless! The ecologists merely echo the words of God, in the beginning, when he told Adam and Eve, "Take good care of all the things I have made."

One of the worst counterfeits of all is what man has done with God's most precious gift of all—ourselves. Down through the ages, men and women (the crown of God's creation) have been disgraced and degraded beyond our wildest imagination.

...Slaves were often treated like animals (beaten, burned, and buried in nameless graves).

...Minorities have been persecuted all over the world (tortured, gassed, shot, hung, and ridiculed unmercifully).

...Newborn babies have been thrown into rivers and abandoned in trash heaps.

...Little children and old people have innocently suffered abuse at the hands of cruel families.

...Mental patients have been hidden in back rooms and institutions with no therapy or hope of ever getting out.

...Prisoners have languished in their cells, unrehabilitated and forgotten by their keepers.

...Men and women have sold their bodies cheaply and expensively to satisfy the lust of others.

...Millions push pills, shoot dope, and drink alcohol until their bodies and minds are wasted and warped.

What does God think of all this? What do you think of all this? What is God's solution to ugliness? What is yours?

God counters with beauty—for that is God's way.

...He inspired the slaves with his very presence. He taught them how to sing and pray and trust in him. He told them how to serve their masters and how to do their work as unto the Lord. He comforted them in their tears, in their weariness, and in their pain. He sent men to "free" them from their bondage.

...Whenever God's people are a minority, he is in the midst of them. When they are persecuted, he tells them what to say. When they are called into martyrdom, he walks with them into lion's dens, burning furnaces, up the gallows, and in front of the firing squad.

...When babies have no home, he raises up adoption and placement agencies so that thousands of homeless children can grow up in a real family.

...When little ones and older ones suffer abuse, he raises up people who build and staff hospitals, orphanages, and nursing homes. He inspires organizations who appeal to distraught parents via TV to "Come for help—before you hurt a member of your own family."

...When mentally and emotionally sick people feel like they'll never get well—God raises up doctors, nurses, and therapists who say, "Yes, you will! Let me help you! Let me show you how!"

...When prisoners turn their faces towards the wall, God sends a Corrie ten Boom or a Chuck Colson into their cells with a message of forgiveness and reconciliation.

...When men and women have no respect for the beauties and blessings of their sexuality, God sends men upon the scene like Josh McDowell who shares God's "Secrets of Loving" via the lecture platform and on TV. Christian youth camps and conference speakers spend entire summers preparing young people for the joys of marriage. Many pastors and Bible study teachers devote a lot of time to marriage enrichment. "Marriage Encounter" weekends provide opportunities for indepth growth in loving communication.

...When the drug addict and alcoholic need help, God has his compassionate "angels in disguise" waiting to pick them up. The work of Teen Challenge and Alcoholics Anonymous will surely go down in history. The same is true for the recently formed Suiciders Anonymous on our church campus.

If God can counteract the "ugliness" of life with his "beautiful plans," so can we—because we are extensions of his arms here on earth.

...we can speak up for the minorities and see that they receive their equal rights (by our actions as well as our words).

...We can serve or volunteer in the institutions and organizations that help care for little children, older people, the mentally ill, and prisoners.

...we can encourage our children and friends to attend camps and conferences that deal with the love relationship between husband and wife.
...we can take our children to positive movies and programs that deal with the dignity of man.
...we can read stories and magazine articles at the dinner hour, which focus on man's goodness to his fellow men.
...we can enjoy family life as we celebrate God's beauties together.

Outshine and outweigh "ugliness" with God's "beautiful alternatives." Be a gentle persuader wherever you are, wherever you go. Show the world there is a better, happier, more beautiful way to live!

If we do our part in counteracting violence with tenderness, cruelty with compassion, and ugliness with beauty, then we will help spread "gentleness" across the face of this earth. We will grow old gracefully like the writer of our opening prayer, and we will have made an *impact* upon the kind of a world in which my friend's husband died. You and I can really help change the tide! Let's get going!

> Fix your thoughts on what is true and good and right. Think about things that are pure and lovely, and dwell on the fine, good things in others. Think about all you can praise God for and be glad about [Phil. 4:8].

Ask Jesus to fill you with the fruit of his Holy Spirit so you can live in *his gentleness* and let it overflow onto others.

NINE
Taste the Fruit of SELF-CONTROL

I love you!
I shed my own blood for you to make you clean.
You are new, so believe it is true!
You are lovely in my eyes, and I created you just as you are.
Do not criticize yourself or get down for not being perfect in your own eyes.
This leads only to frustration.
I want you to trust me, one step, one day at a time.
Dwell in my power and my love.
And be free—be yourself!
Don't allow other people to run you.
I will guide you if you'll let me.
Be aware of my presence in everything.
I give you patience, joy, and peace.
Look to me for answers.
I am your Shepherd, and I will lead you.
Take your eyes off yourself! Look only at me!
I will lead you, I will change you, I will make you a new person, but not when you are trying to do it yourself.
I won't fight your efforts.
You are mine. Let me have the joy of making you like Christ.
Let me love you!
Let me give you joy, peace, and kindness.
No one else can! Don't you see?

Your only command is to look to me and me only!
Never to yourself and never to others.
I love you.
Do not struggle, but relax in my love.
I know what is best and will do it in you.
How I want freedom to love you freely!
Stop trying to be, and let me make you what I want you to be.
My will is perfect!
My love is sufficient!
I will supply all your needs!
Look to me!
I love you,

Your Heavenly Father

Can you imagine that this "love letter" from God is sent to you personally? Can you believe that everything he says in it is true? Can you agree:

...that he wants to make you clean and new?
...that you are lovely in his eyes?
...that he wants you to dwell in his power and love?
...that you are free to be yourself?
...that he gives you patience, joy, peace, and kindness?
...that he is your Shepherd and wants to make you like Christ?

I received this precious "love letter" from a friend on the East Coast just at the close of our teaching series on the Holy Spirit. It seemed to sum up perfectly all we had been learning from the Scriptures. I felt it would do the same for the readers of this book. It reminds me of the writings of Francis J. Roberts in her little book, *Come Away, My Beloved*. If you want to enrich your daily devotional life, I recommend you add this little gem. It will bless your heart and make you feel truly loved.

I hope and pray that during our time together in these last eight chapters you have felt the Divine Lover's arms embrace you many times:

...telling you he loves you very much!
...telling you he wants to fill you with joy!
...telling you he wants to flood you with peace!

...telling you he wants to touch you with patience!
...telling you he wants to bless you with kindness!
...telling you he wants to anoint you with goodness!
...telling you he wants to empower you with faithfulness!
...telling you he wants to surprise you with gentleness!

And now comes that final "heavenly hug" ... telling us he wants to fill us with the fruit of self-control.

And we say, "Oh, Lord, that's a tough one! No wonder you saved that one 'til last!" But he answers, "Not as tough as you might think; for if you do as I say in my 'love letter,' then all the hard work falls on me."

Give God:
...your attitudes.
...your reactions.
...your responses.

And watch what happens! You won't recognize yourself at first and people will begin to say, "What's gotten into you?" Be sure to tell them *who* has gotten into you. Tell them about the "great exchange" that took place when you decided to make Jesus the Lord of your life as well as the Savior of your soul. Share God's "secrets of living" with your family and friends. Tell them it's a "free gift" if they'll ask and receive. He'll never turn anyone down.

There is no way you can become *self*-controlled if you're not first *Christ*-controlled, and there's no way you can become Christ-controlled unless you give the Holy Spirit permission to take over your life. Then you can say with Brother Paul:

> I myself no longer live, but Christ lives in me. And the *real life* I now have within this body is a result of my trusting in the Son of God who loved me and gave himself for me [Gal. 2:20].

And then the heavenly Father adds this precious postscript:

> I advise you to obey only the Holy Spirit's instructions. He will tell you where to go and what to do. . . . [and] when the Holy Spirit controls our lives he will produce . . . love, joy, peace, patience, kindness, goodness, faithfulness, gentleness and self-control [Portions of Galatians 5].

We say, "But wait a minute Lord, we're not totally clear on how all this happens—

Who is the Holy Spirit?
How does he come?
What does he do?
What do I have to do?"

And the Lord answers:

> If you love me, obey me; and I will ask the Father and he will give you another Comforter, and he will never leave you. He is the Holy Spirit, the Spirit who leads [you] into all truth. The world at large cannot receive him, for it isn't looking for him and doesn't recognize him. But you do, for he lives with you now and some day shall be in you! When I come back to life again, you will know that I am in my Father, and you in me, and I in you [Portions of John 14:15-20].

"We begin to undersand, Lord. You say you want to live *in* us, but how do you get *in* us?"

The Lord reminds us of a conversation he had with a religious leader named Nicodemus who asked the same sort of question. Listen to the Lord's answer.

> Unless one is born of water and the Spirit, he cannot enter the Kingdom of God. Men can only reproduce human life, but the Holy Spirit gives new life from heaven [John 3:5, 6].

We are overwhelmed with his answer. Like the disciples in the Upper Room, we can hardly comprehend the magnitude of what he is saying. Like Philip and Thomas, we have some questions we want to ask. We need to get very personal, so at this point I want you to join me for an "Upper Room experience" with our Lord. (Put you name and your situation in the context of our conversation and listen for his still small voice to speak.)

Us: "Lord, are you sure you want us? We've made lots of mistakes and we've failed many times. Why we don't even keep all your rules. We're really not very worthy!"

The Lord: Oh yes, you are! My Father's unchanging plan has always been to adopt you into his family, and I've taken away all your sins through my blood. . . . Because of what I did for you, you have become a *gift* that my Father delights in (Portions of Ephesians 1).

Us: "Who, us,—Lord we are a 'gift'? How can that be? Why would God want us?"

The Lord: Because, "I chose you [and] I appointed you to go and produce lovely fruit" (John 15:16).

Us: "But Lord, don't you remember? We've got all these hang-ups. We're not perfect. How can we produce fruit?"

The Lord: Because, "I am the vine and you are the branches. Whoever lives in me and I in him shall produce a large crop of fruit. For apart from me, you can't do a thing" (John 15:5).

Us: "Lord, we'd like to do that, we really would; but *how* do we live *in* you? What does that mean?"

The Lord: Let me explain. "When you obey me you are living in my love, just as I obey my father and live in his love. I have told you this so that you will be filled with my joy. Yes, your cup of joy will overflow!" (John 15:10, 11).

Us: "Are you saying that when we obey you we are living *in* your love?"

The Lord: You're getting the idea! "So take care to live in me, and let me live in you. For a branch can't produce fruit when severed from the vine. Nor can you be fruitful apart from me" (John 15:4).

Us: "Oh, Lord, don't let us willfully disobey you anymore. Keep us rooted in your love. Take control of us, please!"

The Lord: I already have, for you see, sin's power over you was broken when you became a Christian and became a part of me. Through my death, the power of your sinful nature was shattered (your evil desires were nailed to the cross). Your old sin-loving nature was buried with me. When the Father brought me back to life again, you were given a wonderful new life to enjoy—you share this new life with me. So give yourselves completely to the Father—every part of you. Be tools in his hands to be used for his good purposes (Portions of Romans 6). Remember, "God is at work within you, helping you want to obey him, and then helping you do what he wants" (Phil. 2:13).

Us: "That sounds wonderful, Lord! Help us believe that in

the depths of our being. When we are tempted to usurp your controls, give us a way out."

The Lord: I will, for you see, "The wrong desires that come into your life aren't anything new and different. Many others have faced exactly the same problems before you. And no temptation is irresistible. You can trust God to keep the temptation from becoming so strong that you can't stand up against it, for he has promised this and will do what he says. He will show you how to escape temptation's power so that you can bear up patiently against it" (1 Cor. 10:13).

Us: "But how will you do this Lord? How will you help us escape?"

The Lord: Very simply. By following after the Holy Spirit, you will find yourselves doing those things that please God. Following after the Holy Spirit leads to life and peace. So you have no obligations whatever to your old sinful nature to do what it begs you to do. Through the power of the Holy Spirit you [can] crush [temptation] and its evil deeds. For all who are led by the Spirit of God are sons of God—God's very own children, adopted into the bosom of his family and calling to him Father, Father (Portions of Romans 8).

Us: "Oh Lord, keep talking. It's making more and more sense . . .

. . . anyone who *calls* upon your name will be saved [Rom. 10:13].

. . . all who *receive* you have the right to become children of God [John 1:12].

. . . when we are *baptized* in your name for the forgiveness of our sins, then we shall receive the gift of the Holy Spirit [Acts 2:38].

. . . the *Holy Spirit speaks* to us deep in our hearts and tells us we are really God's children [Rom. 8:16]."

The Lord: That's right. You have been baptized into my Body by the Holy Spirit. The Holy Spirit displays God's power through each one of you, as a means of helping the entire church. God gives you many kinds of special abilities but it is the same Holy Spirit who is the source of them all (Portions of 1 Corinthians 12).

The whole Body is fitted together perfectly and each part in its own special way helps the other parts so that the whole Body is healthy and growing and full of love (Portions of Ephesians 4).

Us: "But Lord, it doesn't always work out that way. Sometimes parts of your Body pull in opposite directions. Unless you are in control of our attitudes, reactions, and responses, we can sure make a mess out of things."

The Lord: How true! "Your attitudes and thoughts must be constantly changing for the better. Yes, you must be a new and different person, holy and good. Clothe yourself with this new nature" (Eph. 4:23, 24). "Your attitude must be like my own, for I, the Messiah, did not come to be served, but to serve, and to give my life as a ransom for many" (Matt. 20:28).

Us: "Amen, Lord! How can we let you control our reactions and responses, too?"

The Lord: Come with me in your Bible to Romans 12 and we'll go through that power-packed chapter verse by verse. It is filled with wonderful ideas for *Christian response.* You might want to post this "Adventuresome Agenda" on the inside of your front door to remind you that your heart and home can become a "Response and Renewal Center" for yourself and others.

Us: "R and R (response and renewal) . . . Hey, we like that! Show us how to get started, Lord."

The Lord: Well, first you:

1. *Give me your body:* Let me live my life through you. Let me see through your eyes, listen through your ears, speak through your lips, touch through your hands, and love through your heart. Also, take good care of your body so that I can use it effectively and efficiently for a long time (verse 1).

2. *Give me your mind:* Let me give you an "attitude transplant" so your reactions can be "spirit-controlled." Then you can be a new and different person with a freshness in all you do and think. You'll discover that God's ways really satisfy! (verse 2).

3. *Accept the gift of faith*: The Father wants to fill you with faith. Open your heart and receive. Respond to his

gift and let it renew your soul (verse 3).

4. *Take your place in my Body:* Just as there are many parts to your bodies, so it is with my Body. You are all parts of it, and it takes everyone of you to make it complete, for you each have different work to do so you belong to each other and each needs all the others (verses 4 and 5).

5. *Discover your gift:* Every one of my children receive at least one "gift" (an inborn talent). You are to use it for the glory of God. Some will be called to:

...speak a word for God
...serve others
...teach
...preach
...share your money
...administrate
...comfort with Christian cheer

Under each one of these categories are a host of other possibilities. Everybody can "serve" and "comfort" and some of you can do many more (verses 6-8).

6. *Hate evil and love good* (verse 9).

7. *Really love and honor one another with brotherly affection* (verse 10).

8. *Serve enthusiastically* (verse 11).

9. *Be patient in trouble and pray always* (verse 12).

10. *Invite God's children over for dinner and to spend the night* (verse 13).

11. *Bless those who mistreat you* (verse 14).

12. *Share each other's happiness and sorrow* (verse 15).

13. *Don't act big or try to impress famous people* (verse 16).

14. *Enjoy the company of ordinary folks* (verse 17).

15. *Don't quarrel* (verse 18).

16. *Never take revenge* (verse 19).

17. *Control evil by doing good* (verse 20).

What do you think of that list of responses? Do you agree? Is this the best way to live?

Us: "Oh Lord, you know it is! That's the way you lived your life here on earth and that's the way we want to live our life too. We know we can never do it on our own, but with you inside us we'll bring forth a bountiful harvest."

I hope you've benefited from this "Upper Room experience" as much as I have. It's been a blessing for me to ask the Lord all these questions and listen to his many answers from Scripture. Ask Jesus to fill you with the fruit of his Holy Spirit so you can respond to his controls and let him live his life through you.

In closing, I just want to share with you where I am this very moment in my walk with the Lord. I am sitting on the beach watching a little boy and girl building sand castles, two teenagers playing beach ball, and fishermen casting their lines out to sea. It reminds me of all the stages in my life.

...daydreaming as a little child.
...playing games as a teenager.
...fishing for Jesus as an adult.

And as I look out across the ocean to the horizon and watch the boats disappear into the distance, I realize that life is like this. We sail along in our little "earth boats" until it's time to cross over onto the other side. But what an assurance to know that Jesus is the Captain of our ship and that his Holy Spirit is our "permanent life preserver" for every storm of life.

This morning during my devotions on the cliff, I watched the sea gulls drifting overhead—not struggling to flap their wings all the time—just resting on the wind. I thought how wise they are. I had spent twenty-six years flapping my wings and fighting to fly, when all I had to do was rest in the Holy Spirit's power.

Now as I watch the surfers ride the waves, I realize there is a rhythm built into all of life and if we learn to "ride with it" we will be carried safely into shore. But I've also learned that the fallen surfer gets up and goes back for more, and so can we. God can use the spills and wipe-outs in life to draw us closer to him if we'll just let him. So don't ever give up and quit. God never gives up on us. Don't turn your back on his love and mercy. God thinks you are mighty special and so do I!

Supplementary Material for Individual Study

In this section you will find study sheets for each chapter and a special "letter" from your loving Father.

The study sheets may be used individually, or they may be used as discussion starters for group study. They'll help you focus in on things in your life to thank God for, and things to ask God's help in overcoming.

Take time to read and meditate on the "letter" at the end of this section. God's love for us as individuals is greater than anything we can imagine! He's only waiting for an opportunity to bless us and shower us with his gifts, one of which is the fruit of his Spirit.

Don't wait. Reach out today. Open up and let your Father love you the way he wants to. You'll never regret it!

SUPPLEMENTARY MATERIAL

Reader's Page on
LOVE

I. Have you experienced God's divine love in your life?
- ☐ Yes, I feel like God's "special child."
- ☐ No, I still feel unworthy of God's love. (Reread Romans 7 and 8.)
- ☐ No, I'm afraid to let God love me. (Reread Ephesians 1, 2, and 3.)

Write out John 3:16, 17 and put *your name* where it says "world" and "whosoever."

II. Check the ways that God's love is being expressed through your life.
- ☐ My love is positive.
- ☐ My love builds people up.
- ☐ My love is unconditional.
- ☐ My love compliments.
- ☐ My love forgives.
- ☐ My love heals.
- ☐ My love is patient.
- ☐ My love asks the right questions.
- ☐ My love is profoundly simple.
- ☐ My love never gives up.

III. Write out 1 Corinthians 13:4-7 and put *your name* wherever it says "love."

Reader's Page on JOY

I. Have you experienced God's divine joy in your life?
- ☐ Yes, I have felt *joy* in the midst of my sorrow. (Reread John 14, 1 Corinthians 15, and 2 Corinthians 5.)
- ☐ Yes, I have felt *joy* when my guilt was forgiven. (Reread 1 John 1:9, Psalms 51 and 32.)
- ☐ Yes, I have felt *joy* when I was obedient to God's Word. (Reread John 15 and 16.)

II. Is God's joy being expressed throughout your home life? (Check the squares that apply to your family.)
- ☐ Daily devotions (sets the stage for our day).
- ☐ Healthy foods (help us feel better and enjoy life more).
- ☐ Uplifting conversations (increases our enjoyment of one another).
- ☐ Completed jobs (fill us with pride and joy).
- ☐ Positive TV selections (bring us positive satisfaction).
- ☐ Family recreation (adds to our pleasure).
- ☐ Friendships (open avenues of sharing).
- ☐ Hospitality (warms our hearts).

(Read Romans 12, 1 Corinthians 12, and Ephesians 4.)

Reader's Page on
PEACE

I. Have you experienced God's divine peace in your life?
- ☐ Yes, I know what it is like to enjoy a *personal peace* with myself.
- ☐ Yes, I am well acquainted with the blessings of *horizontal peace* within the Family of God.
- ☐ Yes, I am experiencing a *vertical peace* of restored harmony with my heavenly Father—thanks to Jesus!

II. Is God's peace being expressed through your life in the following areas? (Check the appropriate squares.)
- ☐ I have peace in my thoughts (mental health).
- ☐ I have peace in my heart (emotional health).

When life throws me a curve, I remember to:
- ☐ pray.
- ☐ thank God.
- ☐ trust God.

God has healed me in the following areas: (mark an X)
God is working on me in the following areas: (mark an O)
- ☐ in my family life.
- ☐ in my neighborhood.
- ☐ in my work situation.
- ☐ in my church activities.
- ☐ in my attitude about accepting responsibility.
- ☐ in my attitude about those who have hurt me.
- ☐ in my attitude about illness.
- ☐ in my attitude about old age.
- ☐ in my attitude about death.

Look up all the Bible verses you can find on *fear* and *peace*. Write them on index cards and keep them in a card catalogue for future reference. Be sure to include Philippians 4:6, 7 and Colossians 2:6, 7. Memorize Galatians 5:22, 23.

Reader's Page on
PATIENCE

I. Have you experienced God's divine patience in your life?
- ☐ Yes, I have experienced God's patience in the raising of my family.
- ☐ Yes, I have experienced God's patience as I face the inconsistencies of life.
- ☐ Yes, I have experienced God's patience in helping me to accept my limitations.
- ☐ Yes, I have experienced God's patience in dealing with people.
- ☐ Yes, I have experienced God's patience in the rough times of life.

II. Is God's patience being expressed through you in the following situations?
- ☐ When my children make a mistake.
- ☐ When my schedule is interrupted.
- ☐ When somebody falsely accuses a member of my family.
- ☐ When my neighbor brags about all their possessions.
- ☐ When someone in the family gets sick and needs my daily attention.
- ☐ When I am confined to bed and can't keep up the house.
- ☐ When people won't do their fair share of the work.
- ☐ When people are unable to control their passions.
- ☐ When I'm out of work with no income.
- ☐ When I'm living with the problem of alcoholism or drug addiction.

Read Proverbs every month (one chapter per day). Study Ephesians 4, 5, and 6 together with 1 Peter 3, 4, and 5. Memorize 1 Corinthians 13:4-7 and Psalm 37:4, 5 and 23-26. Put Romans 5:3-5 and James 1:2-4 on an index card in your card catalogue. Tape 2 Peter 1:2-11 to your mirror or cupboard door.

Reader's Page on
KINDNESS

I. Have you experienced God's divine kindness in your life?
- ☐ Yes, I know from personal experience that God's kindness is filled with "generous gifts."
- ☐ Yes, I agree that God's kindness fills me with praise.
- ☐ Yes, I've seen God's kindness break down barriers between people of different races, different creeds, and different backgrounds.

II. Is God's kindness being expressed through you in the following relationships?
- ☐ Between my mate and myself.
- ☐ Between my children and myself.
- ☐ Between my relatives and myself.
- ☐ Between my friends and myself.
- ☐ Between my neighbor and myself.
- ☐ Between strangers and myself.
- ☐ Between enemies and myself.

(List ten attributes that attracted you to some of the persons on this list.)

III. List 20 "serendipities" God has blessed you with in this past year. (Thank God for his kindness to you.)

Reread Proverbs 31, Psalm 128 and the stories of Ruth, the Good Samaritan (Luke 10), Joseph (Genesis 37-50), and the Prodigal Son (Luke 15). Then write your own "Parable of Kindness" (using personal illustrations from your own life).

Reader's Page on *GOODNESS*

I. Have you experienced God's divine goodness in your life?
   - ☐ Yes, I agree that God came to make me good and keep me good (salvation and sanctification).
   - ☐ Yes, I agree that when I am good (obey God's laws of love) I really feel much better physically, emotionally, and spiritually.
   - ☐ Yes, I have asked God to search my heart, test my thoughts, and point out anything he finds in me that makes him sad.
   - ☐ Yes I have experienced God's correction and I am thankful for it.
   - ☐ Yes, I understand that God's goodness is based on mercy as well as justice (love as well as law).

II. Is God's goodness being expressed through you in the following situations?
   - ☐ God's goodness has helped me overcome self-will.
   - ☐ God's goodness has helped me rise above the world's pressures.
   - ☐ God's goodness has enabled me to resist the Evil One.
   - ☐ God's goodness has shown me how to run away from temptation.
   - ☐ God's goodness has freed me from the penalty and power of sin. (My sins were nailed to Christ's cross.)
   - ☐ God's goodness lives in me because I am controlled by his Holy Spirit.
   - ☐ God's goodness is weaving my life into a beautiful tapestry.
   - ☐ God's goodness is enabling me to live the Spirit-controlled life. (To be "God's love with skin on.")

Read and underline key concepts in Psalm 119. Study Hebrews 12 regarding discipline and review James 1 and 2 Peter regarding obedience. Find all the Holy Spirit references you can in John 14-16 and Acts 1-11. Write a paragraph on what "living the Christian life" means to you.

Reader's Page on *FAITHFULNESS*

I. Have you experienced God's divine faithfulness in your life?
- ☐ Yes, I believe God knows my name!
- ☐ Yes, I believe God precedes and follows me everywhere I go!
- ☐ Yes, I believe God has a special plan for my life and I believe he has been preparing me ever since I was born.
- ☐ Yes, I believe God often answers my specific prayers!

II. Have you experienced God's divine faithfulness in specific areas of your life?

Are you aware of God's instructions:
- ☐ in your family?
- ☐ from the Bible?
- ☐ from preachers and teachers?

Are you aware of God's corrections:
- ☐ in some of life's built-in consequences?
- ☐ in some of life's built-in corrections?

Are you aware of God's inspiration:
- ☐ at some mountaintop experience?
- ☐ through some modern-day saint?

Are you aware of God's protection:
- ☐ in counteracting the forces of evil?
- ☐ in preparing you for eternity?

Read all 150 Psalms and underline every verse that mentions the concept of God's faithfulness. Add scripture verses on "faithfulness" to your card file.

Reader's Page on
GENTLENESS

I. Have you experienced God's divine gentleness in your life?
- ☐ Yes, I believe God's ways are the best ways. (I'm arguing less and trusting more.)
- ☐ Yes, I am aware of the "tough and tender" qualities growing in my life.
- ☐ Yes, I am learning to move with the rhythm of life. (I'm more adaptable—less rigid.)
- ☐ Yes, I am giving God everything I've got. (I'm becoming a yielded instrument in his hands.)
- ☐ Yes, I'm letting God soften my tongue and temper and ego.
- ☐ Yes, I've given up my scolding, nagging, and pouting ways.
- ☐ Yes, I've quit making a fool of myself. (I've turned my emotional reactions over to God.)
- ☐ Yes, I'm letting God teach me lessons in the midst of life's daily experiences.
- ☐ Yes, I'm learning how to "feel" what another person is feeling.
- ☐ Yes, God is showing me all kinds of creative solutions to life's challenges.

II. Is God's divine gentleness being expressed through your life in the following ways?
- ☐ Yes, I am finding specific ways to counteract violence with tenderness. (List three.)

  ____
  ____
  ____

- ☐ Yes, I am finding specific ways to counteract cruelty with compassion. (List three.)

  ____
  ____
  ____

- ☐ Yes, I am finding specific ways to counteract ugliness with beauty. (List three.)

  ____
  ____
  ____

Reader's Page on
SELF-CONTROL

I. Are God's divine controls being expressed in your life?
- ☐ through your love.
- ☐ through your service.
- ☐ through your patience.
- ☐ through your hospitality.
- ☐ through your forgiveness.
- ☐ through your empathy.
- ☐ through your humility.
- ☐ through your friendship.
- ☐ through your peacefulness.
- ☐ through your willingness to go the "second mile" (Based on Romans 12).

II. Do you understand how to become Spirit-controlled?
- ☐ Do you know who the Holy Spirit is?
- ☐ Do you know how the Holy Spirit empowers believers?
- ☐ Do you know what the Holy Spirit does?

Record all the Scriptures you can find in your Bible that tell you how the Holy Spirit empowers you to live the Christian life. Memorize your favorite ones and put them on an index card in your file cabinet for instant referral.

I love you

____

(WRITE YOUR NAME)

I am holding you by your right hand. Don't be afraid, I am here to help you . . . (Isa. 41:13).

Long before I made the world, I chose you to be my very own through what Christ would do for you . . . (Eph. 1:4).

My unchanging plan has always been to adopt you into my family by sending Jesus Christ to die for you . . . (Eph 1:5).

So let your roots go down deep into the soil of my marvelous love so you can understand how long, how wide, how deep and how high my love really is . . . (Eph. 3:17, 18).

Did you know I saw you before you were born? I made all the delicate, inner parts of your body and knit them together in your mother's womb. I scheduled each day of your life before you began to breathe. I chart the path ahead of you and tell you where to stop and rest. . . . I both precede and follow you and place my hand of blessing on your head . . . (Psa. 139).

I will be your God through all your lifetime. Yes, even when your hair is white with age . . . (Isa. 46:4).

I will accept and declare you "not guilty" if you trust Christ to take away all your sins, no matter who you are or what you have been like . . . (Rom. 3:21, 22).

Turn from your sin, return to me and be baptized in the name of Jesus Christ for the forgiveness of your sins, then you shall receive the Holy Spirit . . . (Acts 2:38).

Because you heard the Good News about how to be saved, and trusted Christ, you are marked as belonging to Christ by the Holy Spirit. His Presence within you is my guarantee that I really will give you all that I have promised. The Spirit's seal upon you means that I have already purchased you and guarantee to bring you to myself . . . (Eph. 1:13, 14).

Now you can look forward to the salvation I have promised you. There is no longer any room for doubt. . . . For there is no question that I will do what I say . . . (Heb. 10:23).

Now you are no longer a stranger and a foreigner to heaven, but you are a member of my own Family—a citizen of my country and you belong to my household with every other Christian . . . (Eph. 2:19).

When you become a Christian you become a brand new person inside. You are not the same anymore. A new life has begun . . .(2 Cor. 5:17).

Christians have no veil over their faces. You can be a mirror that brightly reflects my glory. And as My Spirit works within you, you will become more and more like me . . . (2 Cor. 3:18).

PERSONAL TESTIMONY

Now glory be to God who by his mighty power at work within us is able to do far more than we would ever dare to ask or even dream of —infinitely beyond our highest prayers, desires, thoughts or hopes . . . (Eph. 3:20).

My Son, Jesus, will baptize you with fire—with the Holy Spirit . . .(Luke 3:16).

When the Holy Spirit controls your life he will produce this kind of fruit: love, joy, peace, patience, kindness, goodness, faithfulness, gentleness and self-control . . . (Gal. 5:22, 23).

Take care to live in me and let me live in you. Whoever lives in me and I in him shall produce a large crop of fruit! . . . (John 15:4, 5).

FRUIT OF LOVE

Love each other as much as I love you. Your strong love for each other will prove to the world that you are my disciples . . . (John 13:34, 35).

FRUIT OF JOY

When you obey me you are living in my love. I have told you this so you will be filled with my joy. Yes, your cup of joy will overflow . . . (John 15:10, 11).

FRUIT OF PEACE

I am leaving you with a gift—peace of mind and heart. Don't be troubled or afraid . . . (John 14:27).

FRUIT OF PATIENCE

Rest in me and wait patiently for me to act . . . Don't fret and worry, it only leads to harm. . . . Those who trust me shall be given every blessing . . . (Psa. 37:7-9).

FRUIT OF KINDNESS

Be kind to each other, tenderhearted, forgiving one another—just as I have forgiven you because you belong to Christ . . . (Eph. 4:32).

NINE SWEET FRUITS

FRUIT OF GOODNESS

For you see I took the sinless Christ and poured into him your sins, then in exchange I poured my goodness into you . . . (2 Cor. 5:21).

FRUIT OF FAITHFULNESS

But even when you are too weak to have any faith left, I will remain faithful to you and I will help you. . . . I will always carry out my promises . . . (2 Tim. 2:13).

FRUIT OF GENTLENESS

So be beautiful inside, in your hearts, with the lasting charm of a gentle and quiet spirit. This is so precious to me . . . (1 Pet. 3:4).

FRUIT OF SELF-CONTROL

For if you can control your tongue it proves that you have perfect control over yourself in every other way . . . (Jas. 3:2).

So remember my child, the wisdom that comes from heaven is pure and full of quiet gentleness. It is peace-loving and courteous. It allows discussion and is willing to yield to others. It is full of mercy and good deeds. It is whole-hearted and straight-forward and sincere. Those who are peacemakers will plant seeds of peace and reap a harvest of goodness . . . (Jas. 3:17, 18).

So go and make disciples of all nations. . . . Teach them to obey all the commands I have given you. And be sure of this—that I am with you always, even to the end of the world . . . (Matt. 28:19, 20).

Bless you, my child,
your Father,
Savior, and
Holy Comforter